The Theatre of Donald Oenslager

Tristan and Isolde, Finale

Donald M. Oenslager

THE THEATRE OF
DONALD OENSLAGER

Wesleyan University Press

MIDDLETOWN · CONNECTICUT

Library of Congress Cataloging in Publication Data

Oenslager, Donald, 1902–1975.
　　The Theatre of Donald Oenslager.

　　"Productions designed by Donald Oenslager": p.
　　1. Oenslager, Donald, 1902–1975.　2. Set
designers — United States — Biography.　I. Title.
PN2096.04A37　1978　792'.025'0924　[B]　77-16026
ISBN 0-8195-5025-6

for Zorka

Contents

List of Illustrations

The Publisher gratefully acknowledges the courtesy of those individuals and institutions who have lent original drawings for reproduction in this book. All items not otherwise acknowledged have been reproduced from Mrs. Oenslager's collection.

Publisher's Note

No one knows just when this book began. His wife remembers that Donald Oenslager discussed it with his longtime friend John Mason Brown as far back as 1968 — and at once JMB by his own wish wrote the Foreword that graces this volume. The author was not quite that quick; after all, he had more to say, and he lacked (as who did not?) Mr. Brown's rapid facility with the pen. He may well have had the work in mind for many months before he mentioned it to anyone; he certainly spent many further months in preliminary planning and in first textual drafts.

In any event, by autumn 1971 the autobiographical Introduction was written and the over-all concept of the book was well set. Although much remained to be done, the project had matured to a point where a publisher's cooperation seemed needed, particularly in the planning of the illustrations and their integration with the text within predetermined limits of space. The present publisher was invited to participate, and happily concurred.

Thereafter, for a period of several years, there were personal meetings and discussions, exchanges of letters and ideas — on no regular schedule, just whenever one party or the other was moved to meet or speak. Thus a contract was negotiated and signed late in 1973. In the spring of 1974, with general agreement as to the final contents and the physical format, the publisher prepared tentative layouts and put sample pages into type; and some weeks later the author noted that "they have been the yardstick of my writing. . . . I am hard at work on the book and am moving ahead with pain and ardor." Apparently, his efforts to recall details of the earlier productions were slower and more difficult, because in December he reported: "I am working all the time on *The Theatre of D—— O——* . . . and as I approach today it seems to go a little faster. At the moment I am in the middle of the George Kaufman/Moss Hart *Fabulous Invalid.*" By June 1975 he had reached *Life With Mother,* on which he had jotted some preliminary notes; and on the twenty-first of that month, at his summer home at Waccabuc, New York, Donald Oenslager died.

It had been agreed that Mr. Oenslager would select productions for comment on the basis not of their success as plays necessarily, nor of his affection for their producers, but of their capacity as vehicles for his sharing the aesthetic and technical considerations he faced in their creation. Always the teacher, his choices (as the reader will discover) all serve these ends.

It is for this reason, among others, that we invited no collaborator to "complete" the texts after Mr. Oenslager's death; no one else, after all, could adequately provide the commentaries which he did not live to complete.

The volume here presented, then, is the volume that Donald Oenslager prepared, exactly as he prepared it save for such minor editings as he knew would be required. That is to say, spellings and mechanical usages (punctuation, capitalization, and the like) have been regularized and corrected if necessary; one or two discrepancies and factual errors have been ironed out. And, since it was planned from the beginning to hold the text-and-picture treatments within given limits, perhaps half a dozen of Mr. Oenslager's texts have been cut by a few words or even a few lines. In performing these operations, the editor has used the utmost delicacy he could muster. All of his work has been reviewed by the author's widow, Mrs. Mary P. Oenslager, whose gracious and patient cooperation throughout has been essential to the consummation of this project.

Middletown, Connecticut
April 1978

Foreword

What is an artist? He is many things, but among others he is a man who makes debtors of us all by saying to our senses what our spirits need to have said in order to be satisfied. If he is a scenic artist such as Donald Oenslager, he is at once an architect and a painter, a decorator and a dreamer, and the seeing eye of both dramatists and audiences. His settings are not merely backgrounds. They are silent characters. They are realizations and extensions of what a dramatist had in mind. They are the theatre made visual. Optically, they do their own playwriting. Color is their dialogue; significant detail their characterization; form and emphasis are their plot.

Being an artist, Oenslager is more than a man of Broadway, though on Broadway he is one of the most successful and skillful of our stage designers. Spiritually, he is an amphibian. He lives in a world of facts and also in a world of dreams. For twenty-five years, indeed ever since he did the settings for *Sooner and Later* down at the old and much lamented Neighborhood Playhouse, he has been making contributions to our theatre distinguished not only by their professionalism but by their versatility, their rightness, and their imagination. No playgoers who saw, for example, *You Can't Take It With You, Pygmalion, The Doctor's Dilemma, Of Mice and Men, The Fabulous Invalid, Life With Mother,* or the Players' Club revival of *Uncle Tom's Cabin,* can have forgotten the vital part Oenslager played in these productions, or the humor, the elegance, the beauty, the mastery of period details, and the variety of his work.

Although mainly associated with realism and enormously accomplished at it, Oenslager is more than a realist. He is as adept at symbolism as he is at naturalism, and as at home in musical comedy (*I'd Rather Be Right, Sweet River, Angel in the Wings*) as he is in grand opera (*Fidelio, Tristan and Isolde, Salome, Abduction From the Seraglio*).

He is too big a man and too good an artist to be satisfied with doing merely what he is asked to do. He must also do what something within himself insists that he get done. This is the reason for such of his projects as his adaptation of the Book of Job and his stirring modernization, in Arthur Koestler terms, of Goethe's *Egmont.* They are exciting proofs that he can meet the compulsion of his own high dreams while more than meeting Broadway's needs.

John Mason Brown

The Theatre of Donald Oenslager

Introduction

Apologia

I like to believe I made my debut as a designer the day my mother brought me into this world. Which of course is not true. One just did not go into the theatre quite that easily, at least not in a conservative doctor's family in Harrisburg, Pennsylvania.

Every career in the theatre including my own is the result of a rather complicated interplay of incentives, dreams, and chance. No two are alike. The phrase "to go into the theatre" implies for most people something mysterious, something beyond the accepted reality of life, a world apart. To the uninitiated, the stage door to that glamorous world is traditionally at the end of a dark, dingy passage, not easily entered. To the initiated, the stage door is the royal entrance to the inner sanctum.

This book is something of an apologia both for my own contrary intentions and explorations as a designer and also for my sketches, which I hope reflect my search for freedom as an artist and my involvement in transforming the course of our theatre.

Initiation

I was an eight-year-old blackbird — one of four and twenty piping out of a pie in a Mother Goose pageant sponsored by the Sunshine Society in the Orpheum Theatre. Not one of us "birds," all sewed up in black cambric, had ever been on a stage before. My own stage experience was confined to my F.A.O. Schwartz toy theatre. The day of the performance we were led into a shadowy place like a warehouse, mysterious with flimsy paraphernalia hung high overhead. I guessed this *must* be our stage. The rest of the unruly rebels were not as convinced. The professional "lady coach" lined us up facing a drab wall. Our music struck up far away. "Now, flap your wings." Suddenly the entire wall rose magically before us, revealing a row of colored lights on the floor; and beyond, dim and vast, I recognized the Orpheum's gold boxes, balconies, and velvet seats all filled with people clapping. Only recently I had sat out there spellbound before *Rip Van Winkle, The Bluebird,* and Maude Adams in *Peter Pan.* Now on this same stage before an audience, we neophytes were no longer "playing" blackbirds, we *were* blackbirds. All too soon for me we ended up in the pie, the curtain came down, and our number was over — but not my memory of it. That was my first time on any stage. In those brief minutes I was dimly aware that I was acting out on those rough boards some wonderful, new kind of initiation. I was stagestruck! and have been ever since.

A Sense of Theatre

Few recover from their first attack of stagestruck wonderment. Happily there is no permanent cure for it. The inner sense of theatre is a contagious infection. Those who are possessed to the full with this sense of theatre we admire more fully because their appraisal of life is singularly dramatic, highly personalized — indeed unique. Bach, when asked why he was forever playing his clavichord, replied forthrightly, "I compose for the glory of God and a pleasant occupation." In the theatre, Helen Hayes, Bob Hope, Martha Graham, Marcel Marceau, Mike Nichols, Josef Svoboda share the same "pleasant occupation" in the exercise of their imaginations. They possess the power of recall — a train of meaningful moments in their worlds which they once experienced; and as artists on the stage, with gesture, movement, sound, color, form, or light, they can conjure up and transmit to an audience the essence of a mood, be it suffering or elation. Each belongs to the theatre, born to it under a conspiracy of stars.

We cherish the memory of a scene or a dramatic moment in our theatre because a few of those elect mortals, animated with this sense of the dramatic, have created for us the immortal illusion of something wonderful or terrible happening in our presence. Specific memories come forward: a spectacular entrance of Mei Lan-fang in a dingy Peking theatre; the frenzied obsession of kris dancers falling in a trance before a temple in Bali; the Fratellini Clowns releasing streamers of humor in the Cirque Medrano high up on Montmarte; Kirsten Flagstad performing the miracle of converting a Metropolitan audience of three thousand into a single spectator with the "Liebestod"; Katharine Cornell as Juliet in the balcony scene; Laurence Olivier's shattering performance in *The Dance of Death*; or Emmet Kelly searching for a lost friend in the circus. These are crystalline moments in the theatre, yet they are the common denominator of a universal recognition of this "common sense of theatre."

Out of my window eighteen stories above Times Square in the heart of the theatre district, Broadway by day looks tawdry and shabby — like old scenery exposed on a sidewalk naked to the sun's worklight. By night it becomes another more familiar world. Shadows meld with the sky's velvet cyclorama. All is light, color, sound, and motion charged with an air of unashamed expectancy. At eight-thirty Broadway displays an infectious sense of theatre — backstage, out front, along the sidewalk, by movies or cafés, on foot or in taxis. Every heart thumps a little faster. Life is accelerated. Now in this valley eighteen stories down below, all this dramatic excitement strangely recalls to me the fervor of those few vital minutes, "my first time on any stage," experienced so long ago.

I also recall gazing down into another valley, a valley in Greece embracing a classical, sacred precinct. Here too is a dramatic setting. From a verdant hillside two springs gush forth side by side. The ancients called one spring Forgetfulness and the other Memory, and the two springs join together in a deep, clear pool. In some way, within us all, flow these two elements. What we forget yields place to those guidelines we come to remember so vividly. And each generation must subtract from and add to the ever-changing world stream of the theatre. It would indeed be a hollow generation sadly lacking in wisdom that felt no compelling urge to make the world of the theatre over after its own heart's desire.

Dreams and Visions

The theatre has a way of luring you into believing that somehow you owe something to the world. Consequently, in the theatre, you have a present imperative desire to "make believe" in order that an audience may believe. The most compelling theatre artists are those who most implicate an audience. What the theatre artist divines is the measure of his vision, and it determines his capacity to pry open the eyes of his generation.

The heroes of the theatre before whom I lit candles as a young man were Adolphe Appia and Gordon Craig, prophet and iconoclast; also my American peers Norman Bel Geddes and Robert Edmond Jones, practicing visionaries, opening windows on new vistas for tomorrow's theatre. At Harvard in 1920 the latter delivered a vague, provocative address on the art of the theatre. That shy, bearded artist, a high priest in tuxedo, hypnotized us acolytes with his lustrous vision of theatrical magnificence.

In Cambridge I was painfully happy devising sets for George Pierce Baker's 47 Workshop plays, and also for the ambitious Harvard Dramatic Club, whose policy was to present notable plays by contemporary foreign playwrights. Our finale in December, 1922, was an adventurous presentation of Andreiev's *The Life of Man*. This was a searching play of symbol, destiny, and fate, and an obvious challenge to my scenic growing pains to provide an expressive environment for actors and drama. Andreiev's play served us well and even received commendation from the great H. T. Parker, critic of the Boston *Transcript*. He understood the psychological and expressionistic intentions of my symbolic settings and costumes, and noted: "From a Harvard that stifled and under-judged him on its teaching staff went Mr. R. E. Jones to become the ablest of stage designers in the American theatre. After him and from the 'student body' now bids fair to go Mr. Oenslager." Shortly after, I was flattered to receive a letter from Mr. Jones inviting me to meet with him in New York.

Wanderjahr

In September I was off to Europe on a Sachs Travelling Fellowship for a year with John Mason Brown to explore the continental ways of modern stagecraft, rightly called the "New Movement in the Theatre" because it really was new. John recalls those years in the early twenties "when backgrounds for the theatre were in the foregrounds of the minds of many of us who were stagestruck. Scenery was in itself a rallying point, indeed almost a battle cry."

We were impressed with the tremendous artistic vitality of the European theatre, and the peoples' universal devotion to their theatres' culture. During those heady months I was perplexed about the relation of the American commercial theatre to our few art theatres and to our emerging educational theatre.

Jottings in my European notebooks recorded my concern for a way of making the theatre a more meaningful force in our society. The day before we had sailed for Europe on the *Olympic,* Jones wrote down a solemn manifesto for John and me in his cell, high above Bergman's Scenic Studio. A groping paragraph, obviously inspired by Jones, revealed my youthful aspirations: "Lately my efforts have been directed against the complete superficiality and artificiality of so much of our theatre today. I don't mean all of it — I have been trying to work out a new medium that might bring the theatre into a more vital significance in the life of the people — principally by studying the sources of energy that made drama in its earlier periods either so much a part of their spiritual life or a sensitive reflection of secular environment."

Wanderjahr took us from Stockholm to Berlin, Munich, Vienna, and Athens. The theatre we saw and those men of the theatre we met in 1924 gave us new horizons. Maestro Gordon Craig alone failed to open his door to us and by return note recommended we continue studying with "our" American master, George Pierce Baker. Professor Baker had given us our note to Craig! Until he reached ninety, when we finally met in Vence, my only contact with Craig had been a correspondence course.

In Europe I also became very curious about my designing forbears' approach to their theatres' challenge. I began to acquire their drawings for the theatre from the Renaissance down to today. They were plentiful then and cost but a few marks or lire. These drawings form a lively collection which I share with others and from which I ever learn anew.

Changing Patterns

The photographic false façades that adorned the stages of Henry Irving and David Belasco epitomized the archeological aims of the nineteenth century, yet they collapsed like cards before the assaults of Gordon Craig and Adolphe Appia — iconoclasts and self-proclaimed prophets of the New Movement in the Theatre. Later, secessionists from that same New Movement themselves turned reformers. Their work bristled with overtones of Freud, machine worship, and futuristic art. And what has become of their avant-garde style of scenery? They would agree with Sherwood Anderson, who used to say that in America the public was not for the artist, it was not against him — it was merely not with him.

There was unselfish unity of purpose among those fledgling off-Broadway groups — the Theatre Guild, the Neighborhood Playhouse, the New Playwrights, and the Provincetown —

Greenwich Village Group espousing the plays of Maxwell Anderson, Philip Barry, Sidney Howard, John Howard Lawson, Eugene O'Neill, and Elmer Rice. Designers, growing dissatisfied with the limitations of the old theatres, were moving out of the proscenium arch in their quest for new theatre forms. Overnight, circuses and garages and ballrooms became theatres. New York received visits from sundry troupes of the Great World Theatre — Mei Lan-fang, Stanislavsky, and Max Reinhardt were only a few. Each troupe administered its own peculiar antidote for the old realism. Each submerged the American theatre in a tidal wave of stylistic wonder, whether it was symbolism, expressionism, or constructivism.

First Things First

That was the year that Robert Edmond Jones, Kenneth Macgowan, and Eugene O'Neill formed an alliance called Experimental Theatre Inc. They took over the intimate Provincetown and Greenwich Village Theatres in lower Manhattan with the intention of presenting the finest theatre of the past and the present. "We are just a theatre," O'Neill said. "Beyond that let what we do give us a name." Their manifesto: "The difficult is our special task — or we have no reason for existing." All concerned were imbued with their vitality, vision, and idealism.

On my return from Europe, in a dilemma over beginning a career in the theatre, I reluctantly queried Bobby Jones about accepting an appointment on the Harvard Fine Arts faculty the following fall, or breaking right into the theatre in New York, and concluded, "Might there be anything in the Provincetown–Greenwich Village Group?" And in the autumn there I was, with Macgowan, Jones, and O'Neill. (Thus I narrowly escaped an academic refuge, which I would eventually settle for, but on part time, with Baker, after his move to the Yale Drama School. So I went to work with this group as a technical associate, or better, as an apprentice assisting Bobby Jones. On eighteen dollars a week I was the richest man in New York. I shopped for Bunthorne's sunflower and for tired dungarees for the O'Neill one-acts, I made props for Stark Young's *The Saint.* Evenings, in their production of *Desire Under the Elms,* I played a square dancer in a scene with Walter Huston. This Equity chore made me twenty dollars a week richer, but that was nothing compared to the inner richness I shared in the dynamic direction of that tripartite alliance. John Howard Lawson expressed the climate this way: "One no longer need think of the theatre of the future in uncertain terms of promise and hope because that theatre is, here and now, an actuality. To be sure it is not represented in the flesh marts and sombre commercial temples of Broadway. But there is, nevertheless, stirring proof that the dream of a dynamic American drama is gradually becoming a solid fact." All those off-Broadway groups were living this dream.

One day I received a summons to the Neighborhood Playhouse on Grand Street. Would I care to design their next production, a ballet, *Sooner and Later,* by Irene Lewisohn, with music by Emerson Whithorne? This was a dance satire in three parts or "states of existence" — primitive tribal life, dehumanizing mechanistic life, and life in a crystalline state of the future. Designing the past, present, and future was a challenge that might never come my way again — and here it was, my first production in New York. For two months I was immured in Grand Street. The staff of the Playhouse made of theatre craft a fine art. And working with Irene and Alice Lewisohn, both so sensitive and driving with inspiration, was a rare privilege. We introduced Thomas Wilfred's Clavilux for the first time on the stage to project those mobile forms of "the crystal buildings of the third existence." Only the *cognoscenti,* the seers of the avant-garde, applauded those earnest overtones and vibrations of 1925.

What to Design

For the educational theatre that year the score was: Yale–47, Harvard–o. George Pierce Baker had been lured from his 47 Workshop at Harvard to Yale to establish a Department of Drama with a munificent gift from Edward S. Harkness. This dangerous academic experiment became the working model of the first educational theatre in America. At Harvard I had designed workshop plays for Mr. Baker. Now he invited me to join his staff and supervise the work in stage design. At that time there was no method for teaching stage design. I learned to design by going to the theatre, by doing it myself. Now I had to formulate my own ideas for others to follow. I found it a taxing but quickening experience.

That first year in New Haven I had to wire Dwight Wiman I could not design his production of Ibsen's *Little Eyolf* for Broadway because Mr. Baker had "locked" me in my classroom at Yale. That settled it. The following year I returned to New York, and over all the years since then I have commuted weekly to my classes at Yale.

After setting up and lighting a production and the ardors of dress rehearsal, I have found there is rewarding contrast the next morning in catching the early Thursday train to New Haven to lecture on the visual aspects of the theatre and to criticize the work of growing designers at the School of Drama.

Teaching design in the theatre is midway between the practical and the ideal and therefore affords a third area of interest for me. In a university school of drama, not *how* to design or *to be able* to design should be emphasized, but *what* to design — above all, content. Young designers must learn to discriminate; they must learn "how to know the waking vision from the idle dream" — that rarest of gifts, Aeschylus tells us, Prometheus gave to man. Good scene designing is good thinking, with freedom of imagination supplemented by reasonable performance in execution. Essential is a proper climate in which practical experience is balanced by an imaginative approach to the theatre of both the past and the present. This balance implies training facilities where students work closely together under technical guidance.

Often the best criticism may be the student's comparison of his own work with that of his fellow students. In the beginning they are side by side at the post ready for their arduous three years' race. Competition is healthy and essential to their development. But all is not running. Within the microcosm of the university young designers must enjoy the privilege of discovering other worlds tangential to the theatre — stimuli to the eye and to the mind.

In my teaching and my work I have always stood for theatre traditions, cultivated standards of craftsmanship, emphasized the values of style and personal taste, and above all practiced discipline. By my own strict way of work I have insisted that schedules be met, and also that rigid deadlines be met by students. This insistence established the close rapport so essential between designer and apprentice.

Some of those impetuous initiates sometimes found it difficult to follow my brand of theatrical pedagogy. I always badgered the first year student, sometimes dismembered him, and then helped him to discover the full depth of his talent and gave him the courage to believe in his work — and above all, to have hope. Always over the years I have tried to set my courses to conform with the changing compass of the theatre. In this way I discovered that teaching can be as exciting as designing and that learning to design should be as exciting as teaching it.

Much Ado About Many Things

In 1927 producer Laurence Schwab, who had directed some of the Hasty Pudding shows at Harvard, asked me to design my first musical. That was *Good News* for me! Between 1927 and 1937 I happened to design many successful musicals — *The New Moon, Follow Through, Girl Crazy, Anything Goes,* and *I'd Rather Be Right.* During this decade I was fortunate in collaborating with many composers and librettists all intent on devoting their talents to establishing new directions for the American musical theatre: Sigmund Romberg and Otto Harbach, Oscar Hammerstein, Rodgers and Hart, the Gershwins, Cole Porter, Moss Hart, and George S. Kaufman.

The Designer's Role in the Theatre

I soon became aware of the hazard that the designer, like the actor, can become type-cast by producers and directors. He can easily and successfully fall into a routine groove. He becomes catalogued as a specialist associated with a limited area of theatre — the musical, drawing room comedy, or a brand of serious drama. This is unfortunate, for most designers like to associate themselves with all types of theatre. Variation in the character of one's assignments tests his talent, develops his style, and enables him to stretch and mature as an artist.

As a designer I have always planned and executed the lighting for my scenes. I believe setting and lighting are complementary — one and indivisible. Nor should the performers in costume be separated from the world of the setting they inhabit. That is the reason I enjoy designing the clothes for a period play or an opera, knowing that they will be integrated with the total visual and directorial concept of the production.

Sometimes you cannot design in the theatre all those things you dream of doing. Then I turn to designing projects like *Job* and *Egmont 49.* These projects are problems I assign myself. I am my own audience. They are ideas for productions, research and new experiments in media of scenery and lighting and costumes which are not demanded by the average production one is asked to design for Broadway. They cost no more than the pleasure in planning and sketching them. Perhaps they might suggest ideas to a director or a young playwright or a new producer for tomorrow's theatre.

If the designer undertakes too many commissions in a single season he may appear to spread his work and his time too thinly and his producers may feel slighted. In these matters the professional theatre is impersonal and can affect the prestige and the success of the artist's career. The designer must constantly alert himself to the fickle "fair" and "storm" signs of Broadway's ever-changing barometer. Wherever he may work, the designer alone remains his own guide for expanding his career in the performing arts.

The scene designer is a man of many minds. He obeys a

 Orfeo, Set

necessity. He thinks in terms of realism, impressionism, expressionism, and surrealism — all at the same time. The designer's compass of intuition will determine the direction away from reality which the play's production will follow. His profession employs all conventions, past and present, and his art is a fine art of variation. Michael Kustow aptly observed, "Whatever he [the artist] does and and however he does it is an act in search of freedom." The designer asks himself how his setting should look, first to himself, then to the audience. A setting is the distillation of his hopes and visions for the play, the realization of the mind's eye of the dramatist, yet that setting is also the silent omnipresent character of the designer. It is like a still life on the stage and does not come to life until it becomes animated with the actors before an audience.

Post-Depression Gold Rush Years

Broadway responded healthily to the post-depression gold rush years of the thirties. The scenic studios were always working overtime. The second floor of Bergman's rookery on Thirty-Ninth Street was the informal roost for most fellow designers — Woodman Thompson, Lee Simonson, Norman Bel Geddes, Jo Mielziner, Ray Sovey, and many others. Bobby Jones held court in his old gray studio high up in the paint loft. Scenery was delivered to the studio from the builder virgin white and was hauled out complete with a "Bergman bath" with frightening precision. Once Aline Bernstein and I each had productions moving out of Bergman's the same afternoon. Mine was the deck of a tramp ship setting up in a Boston theatre, and Aline was setting up her *Grand Hotel* in Baltimore. My smokestack arrived as a marbleized column, and a section of her hotel lobby was my weatherbeaten smokestack!

I became involved in many challenging adventures in production. There were Paul Green's *Johnny Johnson* and Melvin Levy's *Gold Eagle Guy* with the youthful Group Theatre. Theirs was a solemn circle, self-centered, not rich but freighted with ideals as well as ideas and talent. "The sparks flew upward" in all directions; those pioneering directors Harold Clurman, Cheryl Crawford, and Lee Strasberg, along with many playwrights and talented actors, were unaware they were all headed for prestigious power and stardom on Broadway and in Hollywood.

Shortly I was flattered to be signing contracts for my first productions with those veteran producers William A. Brady, Arch Selwyn, Charles Dillingham, and John Golden; also with Sam Harris, Max Gordon, Vinton Freedley, and Gilbert Miller. They were tough overlords of the big-time era of theatrical enterprise — independent managers of the old school. "Show business" was their tradition. In fact their theatre know-how was so astute that they sought out, tolerated, and indeed projected the ideas of the younger generation of directors and designers. Over those years, through successes and failures, mutual understanding filled me with admiration for their integrity and the formidable professionalism of their staffs.

At the same time I became actively engaged designing with younger producers who sometimes wrote their own plays and frequently directed them. There were also directors who worked only for producers. Among them were expert, meticulous George Abbott; *simpatico,* dedicated Marc Connelly; Alfred de Liagre of impeccable taste; Sir Tyrone Guthrie, with a daemon for invention; volatile Jed Harris (God rest my tortured soul!); John Houseman, with a weather eye for new directions; Garson Kanin, full of fire and flare; Sidney Kingsley, overall man of the theatre; Charles Laughton, intellectual actor with a profound intuition for theatre; Howard Lindsay, mastermind of comedy; Alfred Lunt, of infinite precision and invention; Guthrie McClintic, perennially in love with the theatre old and new; and Herman Shumlin, radiating theatrical insight. Because of their innate sense of theatre, each of these men imprinted his individual hallmark on his production. Naturally his name appeared in large type on the theatre's house boards, but not one of these directors was a "dominus do-all" who like some clairvoyant directors today *alone* conceive the interpretation of the author's script and *alone* bring it to life on the stage. All were collaborators, always susceptible to the ideas of others; indeed they expected the designer to contribute his hopes, his dreams, and his practical intentions for the visualization of the author's script. Each of these producers, authors, and directors brought ordered theatricality and stability to the Broadway scene because they shared a common affection for, and dedication to, the theatre.

Lively Stepchildren

"Affection for and dedication to the theatre" has always implied a passionate love affair with the fabulous theatre past and present, in every land around the world. Does it stand to reason that this same zealous passion tears at the vitals of those guardians of the theatre's stepchildren, motion pictures and television? Within a single generation, sired by technology and born of the living theatre, they have grown into two monster forms of supercommunication. They are as essential to the creature comfort of twentieth-century *Homo sapiens* as his latest juggernaut, the supermarket — all body, no soul or spirit. Via cinematic magic and the air waves of television the world's public is mechanically transported anywhere, any time, in any way, without benefit of the true living presence. Leonardo da Vinci, looking into a mirror, discovered this loss of direct communication in observing that the reflection of nature was once removed from the real thing. This I believe is the great aesthetic divide between the living theatre and her technological stepchildren.

However, I confess that from those nickelodeon days and later after the movies took over my Orpheum Theatre, I have been a movie fan — but only of the finished product viewed from a comfortable seat. When I am moved by a cinematic episode projected on a screen in a darkened theatre, I wonder why I am never sufficiently moved to clap my hands. This lack of personal participation with the performers in their actual setting is why I have never been charmed by the external glamor of working in Hollywood.

Many Broadway scene designers have been tempted by opportunities unlimited in the Elysian fields of Cinema Land and also attracted (and why not?) by financial reward! But most who have journeyed west to labor in a major studio have re-turned home to Times Square as prodigal sons with the same disillusions: "No opportunity for individual expression," "assembly-line control," "design lost in the shuffle of production," "no life in it." Only recently is it apparent that Hollywood's imperial factories are declining in power and prestige. Youth is in. Film students, artists, independent directors and producers are free to go their own way, to make their low-budget films without union sanctions and with a free choice of subject matter and location. At last it is youth, the children of the stepchild, who are discovering their own "common affection and dedication" to the aesthetic potential of motion pictures.

The general laws of scene design are as applicable to the visual conventions of television as they are to films. Born to the theatre too soon, I never thought I would discover much "life" in designing for television — even live television. Yet I am aware of all those talented younger television designers who find employment steady, their work rewarding and stimulating, even with that grinding count-down to the single broadcast performance or to recording that precious live tape.

My first and only encounter with television was memorable for me and perhaps for television. The date was March 20, 1931. The occasion was the first two-way TV-telephone circuit in the world. That experimental program was broadcast from a fabric-hung recording booth in the Bell Telephone Laboratory on Bethune Street all the way down to the New York Telephone office at 195 Broadway, perhaps two miles away. On one side of the booth hung my backdrop, five by six feet. On the other three sides glass panels covered photoelectric tubes whose light was transformed into power, which in turn (like an electric eye) reproduced within the distant six-by-twelve-inch peephole the voice and the image of the head and shoulders of the performer. It was like a large animated vocal postage stamp — marvelous to behold!

What scenic display would be appropriate for this minuscule first? With no precedents and for clarity of projection I devised an abstract design in black and white, a cubistic arrangement of skyscrapers. This dominating cityscape behind the performer created by chance a poetic sepia impression of

New York in a smog and was about as clear as an early motion picture. How far design for television has progressed since that primitive first effort! In forty years memorable visual landmarks in minor and major programs have contributed to the evolution of this newest member of the performing arts family. Designers have developed television methods and visual techniques by taking advantage of the medium's prescribed limitations. However, despite the industry's growing pains and incredible technological progress, should not the sights of visual production be raised higher? Does technology seem to encroach on art? Has the smog enveloping our major cities of television activity penetrated the studios and affected the perceptive eye of the television world? Or is the present-day artist's seeing eye grown a little dim and is it content with its past achievements?

Suppose our skies were swept clear of pollution and the windows of the studios were opened wide to the new breezes of change, opened to ascendant artists of today of the caliber of Giotto and Rembrandt and Daumier and Hiroshige. Think what visual miracles each of these men could have wrought for the television masses of his day! Suppose contemporary artists and directors of insight and humanity were called upon to intrude their ways of observing our world on the proven ways of yesterday's television. Their stimulating involvement could reveal new horizons commensurate with the incredible technological advances of television made by its engineers and scientists in the last forty years.

Designs for the Lyric Theatre

The nagging problems of design in the production of opera are generations older than those in motion pictures and television. Solutions to these evergreen problems have always summoned me to action. There is a definite relation between the musical structure of opera and the plastic organization and design structure of the setting. The spectator should be aware of the relationship of both the continuous flow of sounds heard and the visual rhythms observed on the stage. Schiller expressed it clearly: "When music reaches its noblest power it becomes form in space."

When I first arrived in New York in 1926 I devoted much time to devising a project for Wagner's *Ring*, to be presented not in a formal opera house but within the free space of a convention hall or an armory. My scheme was a single, permanent arrangement of meaningful levels on which all four operas could be played, with fluid changes of locale accomplished by the use of light. Dr. Walter Damrosch, conductor and devotee of Wagner, gave me encouragement and I was flattered that he wanted to participate in the venture. Otto Kahn, distinguished patron of the arts, asked to see my sketches and kindly arranged a conference for me with General Manager Gatti-Casazza of the Metropolitan Opera. In his office on my knees I scattered the sketches for my project on the floor before Mr. Gatti, who in French confided to his assistant, William Ziegler, nothing but appalled amazement over my somewhat unconventional designs. Mr. Gatti was not aware that I, too, had the French touch until leaving his office I politely bade him "Au revoir." I was out on the sidewalk! *Mais tout n'était pas perdu!* Shortly thereafter he commissioned me to design the new production of *Salome* for the Metropolitan's next season. I was back in the Opera House!

At that same time the Philadelphia Orchestra launched its impressive season of operas at the Philadelphia Academy of Music. I was approached to design *Tristan and Isolde* and *Der Rosenkavalier*. This commission would add perilously to my already heavy schedule. I was engaged on nine productions with about fifty settings. Four of them had boat scenes — an Erie Canal boat for Marc Connelly's *The Farmer Takes a Wife,* a streamlined ocean liner for *Anything Goes,* a clipper ship beached in San Francisco, plus a tramp steamer passing through the Gatún Locks of the Panama Canal. I decided there would still be space for Tristan's ship in my busy marina and for *Der Rosenkavalier* too.

For my own pleasure I had already, fortunately, made preliminary sketches as a project for *Tristan*. Fritz Reiner was to be the conductor. Most distinguished singers were imported from Europe. Both productions were to be Viennese Herbert

Graf's premieres as an opera director in this country. We were forced to weld our scenic concepts together swiftly. Fortunately we were *simpatico* and shared "good feelings" for both operas. The scenery was executed in four weeks. Lighting the production during dress rehearsals with the full Philadelphia Orchestra in the pit was exhilarating, and the operas opened exactly as we had planned them. "It is not to believe," said Graf. That Philadelphia season proved that in the United States traditional opera could be presented with the professional standards of Broadway and could utilize experimental techniques in new approaches to operatic production.

Over the years I have designed perhaps thirty lyric works, among them productions for the ever traditional Metropolitan Opera and for the adventurous City Center Opera. Work with the City Center is always stimulating and rewarding because one finds in Julius Rudel and his cooperative organization enthusiasm, courage, and vision. In 1959 I designed Gluck's *Orpheus and Eurydice* for the inauguration of the new Queen Elizabeth Opera House in Vancouver. That was a "splendid royal occasion" presided over by the Queen herself. For another "occasion" I designed Verdi's *Don Carlos,* which opened simultaneously both the new opera house and the HemisFair at San Antonio, Texas, in 1968. Where but in Texas has an opera ever opened a great fair? In Colorado the Central City Opera Festival occupies the stone opera house built by the gold miners in 1878 and described as the finest Temple of the Muse west of the Missouri. For many seasons this old opera house in Central City has provided me an opportunity for experimenting and devising fresh ways and means for revitalizing opera production and restoring the popularity of the lyric theatre among new audiences, old and young.

War and Purdah

Then came those barren years of World War II. My abrupt transfer from my private world of stage design to the defensive world of camouflage was dramatic. I discovered that the temporary characteristics of stage design and camouflage are synonymous. With the same tricks one conceals what exists and by the corollary reveals what does not exist. As camouflage officer of the Second Air Force, I organized and inspected camouflage training programs for all the heavy bomber training bases throughout the wide open spaces of the Middle West. At Scribner, Nebraska, in conjunction with the Corps of Engineers, we camouflaged a satellite training field so effectively that the day following the commanding general's inspection of the field he pronounced it hazardous and ordered that no more flying fields be camouflaged — too dangerous for the trainee bomber crews — they couldn't find the fields! As the war's progress accelerated, camouflage closed its net around me and I arranged for my transfer to Combat Intelligence with a B–29 wing, ultimately based on Guam. Our A–2 section discovered that the accepted method of briefing crews for bombing missions was inadequate, not clear, and ineffective. We proceeded to improve it by simply converting an old theatrical lighting trick into a new briefing aid. In our darkened briefing hall, set up in a large Quonset hut, our maps, charts, and essential target information for the bombing mission were treated with different colors of fluorescent pigment and stimulated with ultraviolet light. This system presented all our information with dramatic emphasis and with the clarity of neon light. General Curtis Le May, commander of the Twentieth Air Force, attended a briefing and was so impressed that he ordered that our system of briefing be adopted by all bomber bases under his command throughout the Pacific. Orders were cut for me to return to the States, procure the materials, and supervise the assembly of all the briefing kits. The day those kits were assembled for transshipment via a "red ball" boat was V.J. Day! But I expect our briefing system must still be in operation.

New Alignments

During those war years all thought of the theatre had gone to sleep. Only once I came to. On Guam late one afternoon the

U.S.O. announced a passing show would entertain our wing. We sat on bomb boxes arranged on a coral hillside and, *mirabile dictu,* along came a flat-top truck with Gertrude Lawrence and Moss Hart playing *The Man Who Came to Dinner* against a tattered "interior" backdrop reminiscent of my original set for George Kaufman's and Moss's play at the Music Box Theatre in 1939.

Amidst this hungry audience, before this improvised truck, with troupers like Gertrude and Moss, I began to ponder how unimportant a role scenery plays in the theatre. All through those days and nights of vigil on far-off Guam I dreamed of a new career in architectural and industrial design. My background and experience in the theatre seemed a logical preparation. After all, Russel Wright and Henry Dreyfus had once been fellow designers in the theatre!

I decided to give up the theatre and venture into a new career. Then one day, while I was still on terminal leave from the Air Force, an old colleague, Richard Aldrich, telephoned me: "Gertrude Lawrence and Raymond Massey are planning to do *Pygmalion* for a new, young producing organization called Theatre Inc. We would like you to do the sets." This crashing proposal bombed me back to my senses and back to life in the theatre. I was revivified, picking up the theater where I had dropped it — resuming activities at Yale and embarking on a succession of productions with old colleagues and new producers and directors who sensed that the postwar theatre needed to go to the bank — not for money but for blood.

Returning to the theatre world of shifting scenes, I discovered many changes. Playhouses were badly in need of refurbishing. I renovated three for the Shuberts. Others were being torn down for parking lots or real estate developments. After twenty-five years only half as many new productions were presented during a Broadway season, for the same persistent reasons that have always beset the theatre: lack of plays, rising production and labor costs, loss of theatres in New York and on the road, ticket prices, and "ice." The intellectual theatre, that bastion of the genuine art of the theatre, was obviously retreating from New York. Other serious producing groups like

Theatre Inc. were making valiant efforts to hold the line. Off-Broadway was becoming the scene of action. I loaned myself to Norris Houghton and T. Edward Hambleton in helping to establish their Phoenix Theatre and installing a unit set in a raunchy burlesque house they had acquired on Second Avenue at Twelfth Street. Their dream was to provide a large audience with the best professional theatre for the least money. All those high-minded efforts to restore the *status quo* on the off Broadway proved futile. The institution of the theatre in our country was becoming decentralized. New alignments were developing between the expanding educational theatre, the civic theatre, and the professional theatre.

International Scene

If I wearied of our own theatre frontiers through frustration or overwork, I made it a practice to travel out into the world beyond the Western theatre capitals — to the countries of South America, to Turkey, Iceland, Ireland, Yugoslavia, and Finland — to see how others make theatre, discover their conventions and traditions, share in the problems of their changing theatre, and finally exhausted, return home recharged for Yale and restored for Broadway.

With these good intentions, back in 1935 I first journeyed to the Far East in search of theatre. In the Chinese Republic I explored the timeless popular theatre of Shanghai, Hangchow, Nanking, and Peking. Sharing a Chinese feast, a few Communist youths confidently discussed the propaganda role that the theatre would play in transforming their world of tomorrow. Peking boasted ten large theatres, ten small ones, and twenty theatre "sheds." The unadorned theatres were Elizabethan in their arrangement. Their thrust stages were bare save for a few symbolic properties. A casual chair played a major role. Actors with the most rigorous training, in fantastic makeup and kaleidoscopic costumes, dominated the casual stage. At dawn I watched young actors fresh from their school exercising, their voices echoing back over the moat from the high, lacquer-red wall surrounding the Imperial Palace of the

Forbidden City. Nearby were the sights and blasting sounds of early morning ceremonials in the red and gold temples. There were the shadow shows, the spectacle of crowded streets, and not least, the universal pastime of betting on cricket fights. For the average Pekinese the crickets were heroes as celebrated as the players of the New York Giants! This vast variety entertainment with myriad changing scenes made Peking one of the theatrical wonders of the world.

In Japan was another world of theatre. I found pleasure in the skill of the last surviving artists of the Ukioye School of theatre printmakers. I sat alongside Kabuki designers devising their traditional scenic splendor right on the stage within the hundred-foot proscenium opening of Tokyo's Imperial Kabuki-za. In Kyoto I became familiar with the hieratic stage conventions, the significance of costume and mask of the Noh Theatre, with the actor Kongo, now titular head of his distinguished family's ancient school of the Noh dance. In the cities the refinement of temple ceremonials and the caparisons and towering cars of festival processions, and in the country on all sides the scenery of Hiroshige prints magically come to life, made Japan a *tour de force* of scenic marvel.

Six years later my wife and I returned to the East — this time to Cambodia, Thailand, and Burma. Each of these nations nourished its own flowering forms of ritualistic dance and drama. Their roots lay deep beneath the cultivation of generations. The theatre of Indochina was one of the oldest theatres in the world — as old as the civilization that flourished under the early Khmer rulers of the ninth century. Watching a performance of this classical theatre, vestigial as it was, one was very much aware of antique ritual and strange convention. One evening through the muffled drumming of Phnom Penh traffic we hurried along by rickshaw to the Royal School of the Dance to attend a performance of the classical theatre of Cambodia. This was the training school for all the performers of the Royal Palace. Those players before us spoke from out of the past with the same voice, employed the same gestures as the dancers carved on the walls of temples imprisoned in the jungles for a thousand years. Cambodian sculptors must have derived endless pleasure in capturing the timeless

beauty of the dancers of the Khmer court. Those tireless Apsarases on the walls of Angkor Wat's ruins rank among the highest achievements of sculptured decoration of all time. These sculptures are witness, as we were that night, to the long line of vitality and purity which the classic theatre of Cambodia had always maintained.

We moved on through Sumatra and Java to Bali. The roads of these extravagant islands of the Indonesian archipelago unfolded in a continuous procession of scenic "spectaculars." In Bali one discovers that the forces of good and evil must ever be kept in balance. Strict adherence to ritual from birth through death is essential to the contentment of every Balinese — to the well-being of every village. Theatre is essential to life. The throbbing music of the gamelan players is ever present, close by or far away in a village kampong or temple court or by the seaside. It generates the rhythm of dance for pleasure, dance for seasonal festivals, or dance for solemn ceremonies, for opera, comedy, or tragedy. Theatre is ever in the air — twenty-four hours a day. You first hear of preparations coming through the grapevine. All this strange ubiquitous theatre we discovered fascinated us. We wanted to remain in Bali indefinitely. Again and again I thought, "If the Balinese only needed a little scenery we might have a possible excuse to stay longer." But they needed no scenery, and fortunately for their theatre I hope never will need any. We carried away a lasting impression of an extraordinary kind of theatrical vitality which the drama-loving Balinese had everywhere generously shared with us.

India is large-scale, and years of curiosity about its architecture, painting, theatre, and people had to be gratified. Recently my eyes and ears were finally surrendered to the charms of India. The country comprises many states, and its visual and performing arts are as varied as the states. In the beginning emerged the theatrical traditions of India. They have ever been an inevitable part of the Indian way of faith and life. For audiences of thousands of spectators there are splendid religious festivals and processions, and durbars are staged on occasions of state. For modest audiences there is everybody's popular theatre. There are the time-honored classical Hindu dramas and dances derived from favorite legendary episodes of the Mahabharata and the Ramayana. This theatre was at one time an essential part of religious celebrations. Today performances are presented in pseudo-Western theatres, or the audience may be arranged on several sides or all around an improvised stage of packed earth or a wooden platform. Lighting is incandescent. Rarely does scenery seem to please the Indian eye. Traditional costumes with masks or elaborate makeup are essential. Performances are presented under various auspices and on various occasions, generally during the weekend. In our sense, India today is not a theatregoing nation. However, important schools are reviving the ancient forms of Indian music, drama, and dance. In the universities the theatre of the West is emphasized. Many amateur and professional groups throughout India present the plays of recognized playwrights of the West. These same groups are also deeply concerned with cultivating a contemporary Indian theatre. Should it spring from the nation's theatre of the past? Can there be a compromise with theatre of the East and West? A number of modern national theatres are emerging — these are courageous and adventurous groups. One eye faces the traditional theatre of India, the other the modern theatre of the West. What new directions should they take? Their theatre must inevitably develop with the growth of the new India.

Throughout the Far East the traditional theatre with but few exceptions is not the popular theatre of today. What is not popular in the Eastern theatre today cannot possibly survive the larger technological drama of a changing society in a changing political world. That is the inevitable tragedy that threatens the future of the classic theatre of all the nations of the Far East.

These working expeditions to oriental theatres are an exhausting and laborious experience, but never disenchanting. Everywhere myth and religion and theatre are inseparable, and the complex pantheons of Eastern gods are not easy for Western digestion. The eyes must fill in when language fails. The age-old customs and unheard-of conventions of the Oriental theatre are a maze of wheels within wheels, but they are ever fascinating to behold. They are a fund of endless values and can provide stimulating clues for new trains of thought and order in confronting the chaotic confusion of our Western theatre today. And in return our Western theatre can offer proposals and help to all of those Eastern countries that are deeply involved in the transitional problems of their theatre's participation in our world theatre of today. The jet and television age has affected all the cultural activities of the world. Increasing these activities ever carries with it the threat of commercialism intruding itself into the performing arts — East and West, North and South.

Theme and Variations

Under royal patronage, Baroque designers were often called upon to exercise their theatrical talents in many peripheral activities. After World War II as a stage designer I was taking on all kinds of extra-theatrical activities. This was the moment when interior and industrial design, store and window display, and packaging too, were turning to the theatre in search of fresh directions. Before long they were "dramatizing" and "theatricalizing" right and left, utilizing our scenic tricks, theatrical legerdemain, and dramatic lighting.

I was asked to introduce showmanship into the conservative Corning Glass Company in Corning, New York. This project for industry was a dramatic presentation planned to promote the potentiality of glass in industry as well as to dazzle the public eye with the full spectrum of Corning products in all their startling variety.

Quite a different project was arranging a debut for a most glamorous debutante — a debut in the world of the arts — a formal public presentation of the newly acquired masterpiece, the Hellenistic Aphrodite, by the Metropolitan Museum of Art. That evening in the dim vista of the long Sculpture Hall Aphrodite was restored to life in a setting of pure light. The applause for that classic miracle was deep silence.

A more "splendid occasion" was the state banquet tendered for Her Majesty Queen Elizabeth and Prince Philip by the Pilgrim Society and the English-Speaking Union in the ballroom of the Waldorf-Astoria. My setting had to be installed within a two-hour schedule — a golden crown amidst stars in spangled order, Baroque candelabra, royal blue table linen, and flowers by Judith Garden. The maître d'hôtel warned me that for lack of space Her Majesty could not be served in the overscale golden Baroque chair in Garter blue moiré which I had provided. What to do — another chair? Out of the question. It was a crisis. "Give me a tray. This is the way to do it." And in the best tradition of Carlo Vigarani, who arranged all the fetes at Versailles for Louis XIV, I successfully served an imaginary Queen to the applause of all the fascinated moppers and sweepers readying the ballroom for the affair.

Only a major incident could propel me into the great outdoors from my perennial indoor routine. In 1960 I was appointed Design Consultant on Lighting and Fountains for the New York World's Fair of 1964–1965, celebrating the three-hundredth anniversary of the founding of the City of New York. Evolving the master plan for the illumination of the Fair, I was exposed to tomorrow's lighting trends still in the experimental stages in the laboratories of illuminating engineers. I was designing innovative water displays with the engineer of fountains, Sam Hamel, and also devising many appurtenances for the Fair's world of tomorrow. This was eighteenth-century theatricals on a large scale, and I accepted Flushing Meadows' great outdoors with alacrity. I came to realize this included one-way visual collaboration with Robert Moses, imperious president of the Fair and inevitably sole arbiter of its taste and style. I discovered that life in Flushing Meadows was never dull with Robert Moses as producer.

Pier Luigi Nervi, distinguished architect of Rome, had engineered a handsome arena for Dartmouth College, which it was hoped could serve as a theatre in addition to housing the college's sports. My commission was to implement this use with a pleasure dome for the performing arts. I invented a demountable thousand-seat theatre, complete with all mechanical and lighting equipment for presenting musicals, dance, and opera. This flexible theatre could be installed within the arena or removed at will. For lack of funds this project remains on the drawing board.

In 1960 Max Abramovitz asked me to serve as his consultant on the interior of Philharmonic Hall, the first structure of the Lincoln Center complex. My primary concern was color. The architect, insistent on perfect sound, urged the acoustical engineers to make their proposals for the design of the Hall. The results are known to all. Nine years later, after two major acoustical operations, Mr. Abramovitz asked me to serve as his consultant again on the (hopefully) final costly renovation of the Hall in the summer of 1969. It was truly a labor of love. Surely this was the most cooperative project ever undertaken by me. Everyone was my consultant! Besides the architect, the acoustical engineer, Heinrich Keilholz from Salzburg, and the contractors, there were the conductor George Szell and musicians of the orchestra, the authorities of Lincoln Center, the administration of Philharmonic Hall, and its President and Board and Ladies Committee of the Board. It was a relieved and joyous cheering section that applauded that acoustical trial run concert. I was happy to be part of it.*

New Theatres for Old

With the exception of Lincoln Center, only the new Astor Theatre (1971) has been built in New York since the Ziegfeld Theatre in 1927, and that theatre has already been demolished. However, many splendid theatres have been built all across our country. Civic and university theatre groups demand the most up-to-date centers. Architects are besieged to fill their ambitious requirements. Architects in turn, for lack of specialized knowledge of the modern theatre and its stage, have sought assistance. Before long I was assuming the role of a theatre consultant to architects. After all, who should know more about these matters than the practicing scene designer? For years he has struggled within those outmoded, ill-equipped, cramped four brick walls that constitute most of the Broadway playhouses built by realtors far more concerned

* But there was more trouble later, and again in May 1976 the Hall had to be done over. — Ed.

Dido and Aeneas, Harbor of Carthage

with the seating capacity of the house than the functions of the stage.

From the beginning I have been concerned with improving the physical conditions of our theatres and with the design of new buildings commensurate with the artistic dignity of our American Theatre. Like the surgeon in his operating room, I am deeply concerned with the architecture of the space in which I work, with evolving new theatre forms, planning the economy and convenience of the total backstage area to include the most innovative and appropriate mechanical and technical stage equipment, flexible lighting equipment and its electronic control, and appropriate sound and communication systems. The stage I think of as my "operating room." For me, stage and auditorium together should have the immediacy of the hospital's operating theatre. This is akin to what I believe the basic philosophy of the contemporary theatre should be — an *Operating Theatre.* I think I came close to achieving it in my plans for the Scott Theatre of the Art Center of Fort Worth, Texas.

There can be no perfect theatre. In my search for the most appropriate theatre forms I have combined historic theatre types with my observations on the trends of European theatre architecture. I have experimented and collaborated on new technical developments in theatre equipment with both theatre and illuminating engineers. And finally I have learned to adjust myself, as a theatre consultant, to the different ways of different architects in planning new theatres for educational, civic, state, and federal programs. Every architect traditionally expects his consultants to adhere to his design. Unfortunately for the theatre, some architects give first consideration to the exterior design of the building (frequently too costly) and thus force the specialized activities of the theatre to function within an economy shell unrelated to these activities. Some theatres are admirably planned but, due to unavoidable contingencies of client decision or lack of funds, fail in the fulfillment of their original high intentions.

Philip Johnson, architect of the New York State Theatre of Lincoln Center, and John J. Flad & Associates, architects of the performing arts complex for the University of Wisconsin, were primarily concerned with the interior functional requirements and followed through with appropriate exterior designs. The New York State Theatre, begun in 1964 by the State as part of its participation in the New York World's Fair, would have been a far better working theatre had the architect been first informed by the State of New York who was to use the building. It was well on the way to completion before it was finally arranged to install the New York City Ballet and subsequently the New York City Opera organizations in this building — too late and too costly to reconstruct the entire backstage area so that it would adequately and economically house their complicated repertory needs.

Edward Stone suffered the same heartbreaking conditions in planning the John F. Kennedy Center for the Performing Arts in Washington. The architect was never informed who would occupy the four designated theatres and how they would be used during a fifty-two-week program. What could he and his consultants do in this dilemma? Mr. Stone proceeded to design the Kennedy Center as a monumental memorial with a long, stately reception foyer overlooking the Potomac servicing three traditional types of theatres placed side by side — one for concerts, one for opera and ballet and musicals, and one for drama. A fourth small experimental multipurpose type of theatre was located in the upper area of the building; it was vaguely programed for motion pictures and visiting performing arts troupes. Each stage was provided with its own technical equipment, and on my suggestion additional adjacent space was left free for future decisions in planning — a costly procedure on top of the staggering increased construction costs of the building due to policy and administrative delays.

Max Abramovitz elected to erect a drumlike building to enhance an advantageous site for the Spingold Theatre at Brandeis University. Consequently the handsome exterior was a *fait accompli* and dictated the interior organization of space. We had to compress into this circular building all of the disparate, highly specialized elements of theatre, including two theatres whose plans could not relate logically to the structural volume of the building.

Wallace Harrison was commissioned to design the urban development plan for the Albany South Mall, one of the boldest and most ambitious redevelopment projects in the country. This ten-building complex of cultural and State office facilities adjacent to the old State Capitol occupies a site of almost a hundred acres. Dominating an axial focal point of skyscrapers, Mr. Harrison created a remarkable abstract sculpture — a gigantic ovoid form 272 feet long and 90 feet high, balanced 22 feet above the plaza on a triple-pronged pedestal. This magnificently engineered object of art and architecture would accommodate a theatre or congress hall for fifteen hundred spectators with the stage back to back with a smaller auditorium for five hundred spectators. Collaborating with architect and engineer on such a theatre was a stimulating challenge, like working on a theatre for another sphere. Access and exit for audience and performers in both theatres are provided via elevators placed within the three supporting pedestals. Forty-five-foot drops contained in a capsule are hoisted through a drop shaft from the loading platform to the stage one hundred feet above. Fresh thinking resulted in an original solution for incorporating the technical and mechanical equipment of a commodious stage house within the total ovoid shape — also for backstage storage space and dressing rooms and the access of spacious stairways and lobbies to both auditoriums, as well as the spatial and acoustical relationships of stage and auditorium. Will this self-contained structure elevated from the noisy world below be accepted as a new contribution to tomorrow's theatre architecture, or will it remain a unique solo effort — inviting the sidewalk chant, "Who ever saw a theatre like that?" In time its use will tell. Meanwhile hopes for a spheroid theatre in a modern world run high.

For Lack of a Proscenium

A few years ago the old Empire Theatre was being demolished. I was walking down Seventh Avenue. The roof and façade of the theatre were already down. The noonday sun glared over the red and gold boxes joined by the proscenium arch of that noble house of Frohman. Within this arch the Drews, the Barrymores, Maude Adams, Otis Skinner, the Lunts, and hosts of others had had their triumphs. I heard a noise like an explosion and looked up. The wreckers' five-ton ball brought the proscenium crashing down forever, and I thought with more than nostalgia, "That theatre is over, the end of an epoch has come."

For four hundred years the spatial conventions of our theatre have been framed within the proscenium arch. In the last generation Urban, Geddes, Jones, and in Europe Strnad, Poelzig, and Gropius shattered the time-honored proscenium arch with their projects for revolutionary theatres. Many of today's new theatre forms are the result of their efforts.

The proscenium frame will never disappear. It will always survive as an accepted theatre form. But in two decades what new directions the frameless theatre has already taken! What Gertrude Stein thought about a frame for a picture is applicable to a frame for a stage. For her, as for many of us in today's theatre, a frame was something to be escaped from — to overcome: "It [a picture] must not only be in its frame but it must not, only, be in its frame. The whole question of a picture being in its frame returning to its frame or not returning to its frame is the question that has latterly bothered me the most. Modern pictures have made the very definite effort to leave their frame. But do they stay out, do they go back and if they do is that where they belong and has anybody been deceived."

Today young audiences find drama on all sides but *not* within our old-style proscenium arch. They believe that the Broadway theatre has forgotten its audience and the audience has forgotten its theatre. They admire the attitude of Thornton Wilder: "The box-set encourages the anecdote. The unencumbered stage encourages the truth operative in everyone. The less seen, the more heard. The eye is the enemy of the ear in real drama." But they must understand Thornton Wilder did not mean to eliminate the designer. On the contrary, he demanded much more of his talent on the "unencumbered stage" — a stage where "action" is centered.

Many free-form theatres have been born of the theatre's changing economy and the collaborative determination of playwrights, directors, designers, and actors to activate more intimately the experience between actor and audience within a common hall. Many modern playwrights insist on their freedom to arrange the audience freely around their play's spatial action. Arthur Miller describes his scene for *After the Fall:* "The action takes place in the mind, thought and memory of Quentin [the principal character]. There is no furniture in the conventional sense, no walls or substantial boundaries." Here is an author in search of a space stage at its freest.

Nothing less can be acceptable. Newer theatre forms are no longer novel. The arena, open, thrust, multipurpose, or themes and variations of all these forms, with the addition of film and television projection are accepted facts of life in our theatre. Yet on water-treading Broadway no producer has erected such a theatre. They are put to proud use by independent theatre groups, the educational theatre, and civic organizations. Off-Broadway they are installed in old movie houses or the Astor Library or in abandoned churches, lofts, cellars, and cafés. And like any underground radical movement these anti-Establishment theatres have mushroomed cross-country. While they are becoming omnipresent, they are not new to America.

What kind of drama happens in these playhouses propagated by members of our young society caught up in the off-off theatre? I fear they misinterpret what Robert Edmond Jones used to say to his younger generation: "Do not believe what you are brought up to believe." They simply "do not believe" and, observing much of their theatre, they would appear to find nothing to believe in while with their own eyes they can see drama happening on all sides. Theirs is the happening without the life of drama. Jacques Levy, who directed *Scuba Duba* Off-Broadway, confided, "I don't see myself as addressing any particular audience. I just do my thing. As for the audience — well, they do their thing." This lackluster attitude of doing one's thing in the theatre mirrors the present dead-end school of total environment in the visual arts. Their sights are set beyond the vanishing point. On four boards, without a passion, tattered actors gyrate amidst constructions of pipes and poles or revel in junk from the dump, while overhead ragged burlap is caught up by tired rope and cruel lights are reflected in distorted metallics. This is the glorious scenic environment of much of today's young theatre in America. It is not the Ash Can School — emotionally, psychologically, and aesthetically it is the Wealth-in-Poverty School, which is tawdry and poor indeed.

What is the preparation for admission to membership in an avant-garde rendezvous of theatre for living — the Performance Group, the London Theatre Machine, Grotowski's Poor Theatre, Café La Mama, Total Theatre, Theatre in the Street? Does admission imply group dedication rather than self-discipline, self-hypnosis rather than deep perception of the theatre's laws, occupational therapy rather than vision?

These are the urgent forces of today's counterrevolt. The ideals and the goals are not apparent. The theatre I first served forty-five years ago was a radical theatre insistent on sweeping changes, but the ideals and the goals were aboveboard for all to see. Jane Heap's "Introduction" to that earth-shaking International Theatre Exhibition in New York in 1926 proclaimed the New Movement's clarion credo: "We are working for the theatre that has survived the theatre. We are working for the sound body of a new society and we have confidence in the strength of newer generations that are aware of their problems. The Theatre is dead. We want to give it a splendid burial. Admission 75 cents." Among artists on all sides was an extraordinary sense of common understanding, organization, and direction.

This solidarity is not apparent in the leaderless ferment of today's generation of splinter groups. Yet today more than ever we need the confidence and strength of these newer generations — to adjust in the areas which were nonexistent. Their theatres-in-revolt are sharing in a culture in which the computer can learn and improve upon its own performance. For how many other occupations should they be training themselves for their future role in society? According to one distinguished authority on urbanization, by the year 2000 (only thirty years away) one-quarter of all people on the earth will be living in cities of a hundred thousand or more. This will profoundly change our ways of life. Our new theatres with their revolutionary commitments should look to tomorrow's responsibility of serving themselves and their audiences in that transformed society of 2000 A.D. Only twenty-five years ago we dropped the atom bomb and that tragedy haunts us today. *The Saturday Review* recently reprinted its original editorial on that solemn event because that editorial foresaw the painful pressures and tragic confusions of today: "If this reasoning is correct, then modern man is obsolete, a self-made anachronism becoming more incongruous by the minute. He has exalted change in everything but himself. He has leaped centuries ahead in inventing a new world to live in but he knows little or nothing about his own part in that world. He has surrounded and confounded himself with gaps — gaps between revolutionary science and evolutionary anthropology, between cosmic gadgets and human wisdom, between intellect and conscience." This is the shattering truth that confronts our world today, and it accounts for the vacuous condition of today's transitional theatre. In today's world our society has created no viable place for itself. The Now Generation's puny theatre is activated by lonely individuals who fail to communicate either their heart's desire or their vision to shrinking audiences. If their theatre-of-revolt under massive leadership had the wisdom to retreat, build anew on the theatre's broken traditions, and then with atomic energy proceed to span these "gaps" with which "[modern man] . . . has surrounded and confounded himself," they could establish a new theatre compatible with the world that confronts us.

Give Me Ideas with Resonance

Theatre feeds on old roots and, like the old and new dispensation, forever regenerates itself, mirroring our changing world. I am confident that from our ashen stage of today will emerge another theatre — a healthy, virile theatre of new-found convictions. In my teaching I have exhorted students to "give me ideas with resonance." I have always aligned myself with the dreams of the Now Generation and for the most part have supported their new-found beliefs. Today where might these

dreams and beliefs be? Vanished? Be patient. Robert Frost wrote to an acquisitive, insecure young writer, "You can see the stars by day if you look down a well that's deep enough." I am confident the newer generation will dig deep enough to see the stars and restore them to the theatre. These dreams and beliefs may communicate an idea to a director, a designer, a young playwright, or a producer for the newer freedoms of tomorrow's theatre. That is what the stage designer of today should care about and search for, believing with Gordon Craig that "the big Dream recurs again and again till it becomes in years the reality."

The longer I work in the theatre, the more apparent it becomes that only the imaginative play projected with the modern theatre's "play of imagination" forecasts the ways and means for our theatre to achieve a new format in the world to come. George Pierce Baker's clarion call rings even more true today: "A drama to be vital must spring from the life of the people and be instinctive with its ideas and ideals, traditions and dreams." More than ever, we must believe in and pursue the imaginative leadership of the living playwright, matching our belief with the playwright's dream — his task of discovering tomorrow's stage. This is not impossible. Lewis Carroll's Queen, on hearing Alice say, "One *can't* believe in *impossible* things," retorted, "I daresay you haven't had much practice. When I was your age, I did it for half an hour a day. Why, sometimes, I've believed as many as six impossible things before breakfast." I daresay at one time the Queen must have been on the stage where make-believe is essential to the audience's belief in the impossible. To believe in impossible things for a half an hour a day would be sufficient to release this world of make-believe from today's straitjacket and restore the discontent of our theatre to the noble traditions of "the Dwelling Place of Wonder."

The Productions

King Lear

by William Shakespeare

A Project, 1924

My first drawings for scenes and theatres incorporated my ideas for making the theatre speak a new language. In a series of designs for *King Lear,* I was moving out of the valley of the shadows of Appia and Craig. Dramatic forms, ascending in light and shade, symbolized for me Lear's tragedy. Those high-flown scenes were quite impractical and heavier to move than the most elaborate realism which I so ardently shunned!

This brief sketch, made in 1924, was fraught with churning ideas exploring classical spatial possibilities between stage and auditorium, for a new theatre of action. In this project for a theatre I was groping with what Louis Kahn in his later architecture would call "the thoughtful making of spaces." Here, audience and performers are caught up in swirling light, enacting a dramatic ritual amidst a runic space of heroic proportions. "Improbable, impossible!" were most reactions. Of course, but so are the dreams and visions of today's youngest generation before they are realized in tomorrow's theatre.

King Lear

The Ring of the Nibelungen

by Richard Wagner

A Project, 1927

The *Ring* was a mammoth production which inaugurated Wagner's Festspielhaus in 1876. From the depths of the Rhine, by way of forests, hut, and palace, to the mountaintops overlooking Valhalla, all was flapping solidity and *papier-mâché,* heavy, naturalistic, and romantic. The scenic style of that first production persisted in Europe and America for fifty years.

One spring, many years ago, I had no special assignment. I was searching for something "big" to work on. I was always a confirmed Wagnerite, but always I saw Wagner's music-dramas with my eyes wide open. Why not undertake a project for *The Ring* and rescue Wagner from his German traditions? The living theatre, to pick up where Appia had left off in America, I believed, must move with the times and reflect and interpret the style of my own age — just twenty-five — and my own time — then 1927 — and must boldly capture the scale of the gods and heroes and characters of the *Nibelungenlied.*

I discovered that the Life Tree of the eddas and sagas proved to be an abstract visual symbol common to all four operas. The Tree sends three great roots deep into the dark, brooding world of Niebelheim. There dwell the three Norns. The Tree's trunk provides shelter to the world of men, even serving as the ash tree of Hunding's house. The Tree's topmost branches rise above the clouds, and are bathed in the radiance of that region where dwell the gods. This region is spanned by the Rainbow Bridge, the one link between the world of men and the luminous portals of Valhalla.

From this symbolic structure I devised an abstract sculptured setting. The gray tones and textures of the structure vary. The lowest areas suggest ancient rune stones. From these bulwarks rise stepped bridges. Their junction supports a final height of overlapping planes. The permanent arrangement of steps, levels, and openings accommodates the taxing technical requirements and scenic demands of the music-dramas.

The action continually shifts from one area of the permanent structure to another. For example, the audience observes the funeral procession, bearing Siegfried's body from the forest by the Rhine, proceeding up over the moonlit heights and descending through the rising mists into the arched Hall of the Gibichungs, where Gutrune, filled with premonition, has been awaiting the return of Siegfried from the hunt.

Combinations of areas, under changing light, assume changing significance. Light welds the dramatic action with Wagner's leitmotif, which supports the plot of the music-dramas. In the finale of *Götterdämmerung,* Brunhilde sets the torch to the funeral pyre that will consume Siegfried and herself. The Hall of the Gibichungs is ablaze as the Rhine Maidens rise on the crest of the river and, with their ring restored, drag Hagen down into the watery depths. Gunther's vassals perceive with awe the flames rising in a quivering cloud bank to consume Valhalla and its gods in radiant light. The musical epilogue of this crescendo of majesty and splendor bursts into the overwhelming harmonic combinations of Wagner's leitmotif.

My *Ring* project was planned for a large auditorium or convention hall. The audience occupies a fanlike ramp before the stage structure at the end of the auditorium, separated from the stage by a gauze curtain, so the structure becomes invisible when the auditorium lights are up. The conductor and his orchestra are concealed under the first tiers of seats — so also are the light, technical, and stage directors.

The prompt book's elevation drawings of the scale model

define the action and indicate light sources and their control for all scene sequences. A portfolio of black and white sketches establishes the dramatic atmosphere of *The Ring*'s significant scenes.

The completion of any project for the theatre is in itself rewarding. But behind the dream of every project is the hope for its performance. *The Ring* did cause considerable interest among producers and news media in 1927; and though it remained unproduced, as explained earlier, it did lead to my designing *Salome* for the Metropolitan Opera.

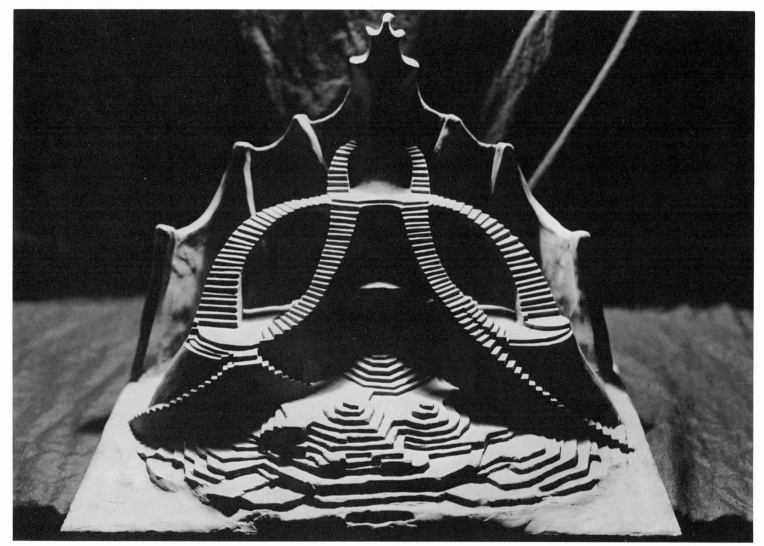

The Ring of the Nibelungen, Set model

The Ring of the Nibelungen, Ascent to Valhalla

Sooner and Later:

A Dance Satire in Three Parts by Irene Lewisohn

Music by Emerson Whithorne
Neighborhood Playhouse, 1925

In 1925 *Sooner and Later* was hailed as the first genuine American jazz ballet. Gilbert Seldes was confident that in jazz America had found an artistic expression of a little of itself. This dance satire attempted to capture the nervous, ironic, and contemporaneous spirit. Its satire was ultramodern — born of the day. It was a virtuoso tour de force which only the Lewisohn sisters, with their long cultivation of the dance and interest in the art of ballet, could tackle with the resources of their Neighborhood Playhouse company on Grand Street.

This dance satire presented, in music, movement, and color, a fantastic slant on three states of existence: first, primitive tribal life with its vital rhythms and elemental human emotions; second, the cross-rhythms of modern city life with the workers driven by dehumanizing mechanism; and third, an existence where the race has evolved into a crystallized state as a result of the supermechanical and scientific devices of the second era.

The twenties was the age of the machine, overriding all other current forces. Artists and musicians, from Leger to Antheil and Whithorne, reflected the benevolence and dramatic beauty of the machine. The machine paid homage to technology, the new god that held the promise of an ideal environment for everyone. It was an incredible decade of euphoria that came to a grinding halt with the financial crash of 1929.

That decade was symbolized in Part Two of *Sooner and Later*. My design portrays the robot man caught under the cogs of unbearable oppression. The scene represents modern mechanistic life where the cross-rhythms of a city are revealed beneath the dwarfing, downward sweep of huge wheels and the dizzy equilibrium of interlocking contrivances. Under a murky sky the masked puppet inhabitants work in soulless rhythmic gyrations to discordant music. Four girls shimmy and shimmy. A factory worker cranks a machine endlessly, a tailor squatting cross-legged cuts baby clothes futilely with enormous shears, and a man in a traffic tower shrieks ceaselessly through a megaphone over the cacophonic sounds of whistles and percussions. The blast of a whistle brings the unfocused movement to a crashing halt, and the workers adjourn to their next scene of relaxation, applauding a gaudy golden burlesque of *The Follies*.

The third part occurs in the remote future. Crystalline workers glide on several levels in geometric rhythms before the changing crystal structures of the "third existence." Four-dimensional settings of light were projected on a backdrop played by the Clavilux, which Thomas Wilfred designed and we employed for the first time in the theatre. These fluid images changed in tempo and movement as well as form and color. Here was an abstract motion picture of the new expressionist art. This futuristic happening took place forty years before the rock 'n roll psychedelic sixties.

In 1925 *Sooner and Later* was a virtuoso experimental work. If this esoteric convocation of all the performing arts was not a smashing popular success in New York's first off-Broadway theatre, it surely received the avid plaudits of the elite public devoted to avant-garde art.

Sooner and Later, The Machine Age

28

Pinwheel

by Francis Edwards Faragoh

Directed by Alice and Irene Lewisohn
Neighborhood Playhouse, 1927

Alice and Irene Lewisohn were the adventurous guiding spirits of the Neighborhood Playhouse. *Pinwheel* was Faragoh's first play in the expressionist manner, and his script excited them. The plot was a tabloid sob story about a "Jane" and her "Guy" in sixteen staccato episodes that swept them from a sidewalk down into a subway, up to a tenement or an office, off to Coney Island, to a movie house or a Broadway cabaret.

After months of heady discussions grafting "the new showmanship" of the expressionists onto the theories of Meierhold, Tairov, and Exter in Moscow, the ultimate production plans for *Pinwheel* evolved. In their direction the Lewisohns would employ a motion picture technique, using spotlights to pursue the stereotyped principals among the depersonalized city crowds. They would invent dynamic movement to achieve visual style in coordinating actors and crowds with sound, light, and setting. The design conception for *Pinwheel* soon crystallized — organic, simple, and clear. The construction with two pivoting mobiles was a freestanding structure wrought of building materials — steel, wood, plastic, tile, and brick, with flashes of red and gold. Varied spatial levels functioned like Tairov's "keyboards for the actors playing."

Behind the construction stood transparent screens abstracted from skyscrapers, among which circulated gray crowds in stylized costumes and makeup. The budget for this setting and all the costumes was one thousand dollars, and my fee for this treasured experience was six hundred dollars.

Pinwheel probably utilized the first clear-cut constructivist setting in New York. In this scene the Jane is spending an expressionistic evening with a Sugar Daddy in a Broadway cabaret. It is a grotesque kaleidoscope of flashing lights, frenetic jazz, and dizzy abandon.

For many in 1927, that radical farrago on Grand Street captured the essence of the New York scene far more imaginatively than the outworn naturalism of the commercial temples on Broadway. On and off Broadway *Pinwheel* roused controversy among critics, literati, and factions of the avant-garde. It brought down the wrath of John Howard Lawson, chief of the rebellious New Playwrights Theatre, for "nothing less than the murder of a creative work." Alice Lewisohn graciously gave the "Revolting Playwrights" (as Alexander Woollcott dubbed them) permission to present *Pinwheel* in their own theatre, or alternately in the Neighborhood Playhouse. Her generous challenge was not accepted.

The hysteria over *Pinwheel*'s expressionism ran its course. Those stormy ventures of the twenties were assertive, clangorous, and full of Utopian thunder.

Pinwheel, Three of the crowd

Pinwheel, Cabaret

Brand

by Henrik Ibsen

Directed by George Pierce Baker
Yale School of Drama, 1928

Ibsen's dramatic poem *Brand* was given an experimental presentation by George Pierce Baker in the University Theatre of Yale in honor of Ibsen's centenary. This was the first complete performance of this monumental work in America.

Ibsen set *Brand* in the wild country of Norway's western fiords, one of those unfinished corners of the earth where the elements of air and land and sea give no quarter in their battle of timeless destruction. Its rugged headlands jut into the restless sea. Its beetling fiords are canyons whose snow crowns are windswept mountain peaks. A gull's cry breaks the silent vastness. In the distance a storm thunders down an abyss; an avalanche roars.

Ibsen made the fiords and snow mountains the symbolic embodiment of the earthly forces Brand was struggling to overcome. "I have never yielded," his echo calls back from the muteness of these rocky walls. Their barren sides are as uncompromising as his relentless "All or nothing."

The many scenes of *Brand* occur in a remote Norwegian community — huts and churches, fiordsides and mountainsides and snowfields. Painted perspectives, projected clouds, and paper snow cannot dramatize the supernatural majesty of these poetic scenes of *Brand*. As pictorial landscapes the settings are not important. As visual dialogue they are decidedly important. Sharp light is focused downstage on all the dramatic action. The settings have no vanishing point to carry the eye of the spectator beyond the back wall of the stage. Perspective is carefully avoided to emphasize the drama of chiaroscuro — all the infinite degrees of grays, from black to white, found in rain and snow and mist and clouds.

Before a neutral cyclorama, profiles of muffled, mourning figures assume significant positions from scene to scene. They loom up like Destiny's ancestors, dramatizing the opposing forces that beset Brand's course. On these figures and the cyclorama are projected stark shadows of precipitous fiords and mountains. On either side of the stage, a flexible wing of overlapping planes confines or expands the acting area and becomes a wall of rock or the roof line of hut or church. Two pentagonal units provide dynamic combinations of acting levels. Reality of plastic form is traded for outline of dramatic mood.

The entrance to the old church is a dark profile of a tumbledown structure that might be found near a remote stave church in Norway today. In dramatic contrast, the new church which Brand has built is suggested by a fresh, whitewashed wall rising up toward snowy peaks. A great cross is sketched on the wall, and before it brood shadows of houses of former days. The entrance to the church is through a radiant light behind the wall. It is the festive day of the dedication, and Brand, learning that he has been a tool of the state, is persuading his congregation to desert this church that is built on hypocrisy and compromise and to follow him to an ice church higher up on the mountain. The setting is the barest means for the fullest effect. The design of a hut by the fiord is only a lighted door. Through a Norwegian hayrick is seen the glossy surface of the fiord with rocky crags peering mournfully into their own sad reflection. The final scene is up among the mountain peaks, rising through mist; the sombre silhouettes of the mourning figures appear in sharp relief for the first time. Brand, stoned and spurned by all but witless Gerd, ascends toward the vision of his ice church high above. Gerd, firing her gun at a falcon, brings the avalanche crashing down. A hollow sound, as of distant thunder, grows into a deafening roar — dazzling light forms rush diagonally across the scene and smother Brand with clots of white; the scene is hidden in blinding light — then utter darkness. And above the roar Brand cries out:

> God, I plunge into death's night,
> Shall they wholly miss thy Light
> Who unto man's utmost might
> Will'd?

Light creates that finale, almost to the exclusion of all other elements of the theatre.

Certain drawings for the theatre have the quality of marginal notes for a script. These designs for *Brand* are only indicative compositions of light and of poetic mood. No design which visually defines the changing conflicts of a play's plot and characters rests secure in completion. A completed drawing means a final statement. The theatre never issues a final statement of a play. In his sketch the designer oftentimes indicates his complete intention for a scene with an incomplete drawing and risks the accusation of indulging in the cult of the unfinished drawing.

Brand, Near the old church

L'Histoire du Soldat

by Igor Stravinsky

Presented by the League of Composers
Conducted by Pierre Monteux
Directed by Michio Ito
With Tom Powers, Blake Scott, Jacques Cartier, Lily Lubell
Jolson Theatre, 1928

The League of Composers was organized in 1923 by a notable group of music lovers to introduce the work of contemporary composers to the American public. In 1928 the League gathered a group of artists together to cooperate in presenting the premiere stage performance in America of Stravinsky's experimental chamber opera for a single Sunday evening. Naturally, salaries were less than minimal. They were token — five hundred dollars for the design *and* execution of costumes and scenery. But the stimulating experience of sharing in such a collaborative enterprise was rich compensation. "For the love of it" was what so much real theatre was about in New York in the twenties.

In 1918, Stravinsky fashioned this opus out of Russian folklore. The theme is one born of war-weariness and disillusion in Europe. A tired and bewildered Soldier wanders home from the wars and sells himself to the Devil. He rises to fame, even wins a Princess, and at the height of his fortune is dispatched to perdition by the Devil. This fantastic work is cynical and sardonic, satiric and civilized. Stravinsky described the opera as a work "to be read, played, and danced." The Narrator acts sometimes as reader, sometimes as advisor, and once becomes the Soldier's double. There is no singing or speaking by the cast of three — the Soldier, the Devil, and the Princess.

L'Histoire du Soldat is a virtuoso work which can be treated on the stage in many ways. For this production, the fantasy of this oldest of legends was emphasized. Michio Ito choreographed the action with mime and dance on a stage within a theatre. On a white drop I painted a distorted, angular proscenium with stylized draperies, a stage box, and a golden horseshoe in yellow, orange, and red. The five inner scenes had the same exaggerated, staccato quality, reminiscent of the *commedia dell'arte,* and were intentionally small to make the tired, burly Soldier appear immense — gigantic in his own capricious world. The costumes, like the sharp-edged linear movement of the scenery, were conventionalized and stiff, broadly painted in bright colors. If one can "picture" music, the settings and costumes sought to picture on the stage the rhythmical dissonance produced by Stravinsky's chamber ensemble in the pit.

L'Histoire du Soldat, Costume sketch, the Devil

L'Histoire du Soldat, Stage within theatre

36

The Searcher

by Velona Pilcher

Directed by George Pierce Baker
Yale School of Drama, 1930

Velona Pilcher served as an ambulance driver at the front in World War I. From her bitter memories *The Searcher* emerged as a passionate, expressionistic antiwar drama. Written in the form of a scenario, the play's realization required time and experimentation in all the arts and crafts of the theatre. In 1930, only a drama school like Yale's could provide students with this opportunity for imaginative learning.

The action takes place in an evacuation hospital near the front, but on which side we are not told. The uniforms are nondescript. The predominant colors are black to white and khaki, and also a little red that comes from flames and flowers and the crosses on the shoulders of the Searcher. The brick walls of the bare stage contain the uncompromising wooden ramp, twenty-four feet wide at the proscenium, which ascends in perspective for fifty-five feet through the back wall's big central door into the shop, where it terminates in the bull's-eye of a target.

There were many reasons for erecting the acting area for this war-torn drama on an incline. The ramped stage creates the illusion of expanded space and dynamically accommodates many scenes. Actors assume added stature. The ramp propels them at the audience or drags them slowly away. It fires the Searcher's explosive speeches into the conscience of the audience. Like a funnel it flares down to a prominent forestage uniting stage with auditorium.

The audience takes its sight along this ramp, which penetrates three circular openings, straight as the bore of a cannon aimed at the distant target. Everything seen and spoken over the cacophony of war appears through the eyes and ears of the Red Cross Searcher.

Reveille rings through the theatre, awakens the audience. The long aisle of a military hospital ward appears in the gray dawn beneath a desolate skylight. Orders are given and preparations made to receive the wounded from the long-promised new offensive.

Several days later, the same hospital ward lies beneath the blanching light of afternoon sunshine. Each numbered bed cradles a body. Straight as two never-meeting lines run the two parallels of pain. The Searcher, working on the Missing List, moves along this aisle, her comforting stature towering above the low cots.

Darkness transforms the ramp into an empty canteen; a shiny screen like a slab of light at the end of a traveled tunnel silhouettes the Searcher stalking down to engage in the military business of censoring her patients' mail.

An air raid comes and goes, and out of murky confusion rise rows of corrugated hospital barracks. Commanded to the victory dance, doctors in gas masks, coupling with nurses wearing influenza masks, arrive for the revel. Under a barrage of rain, riotous bodies surge up and down the reverberating boardwalk in a jazz caricature of an orgy. Suddenly the revelry along the street has passed like the air raid, and so has the rain. The Searcher, silent witness of this mordant ballet, is left alone in bitter despair. A barrage of distant gunfire silhouettes the rooftrees of the barracks, retreating like crosses toward Cemetery Hill, now aglow with white crosses and ablaze with scarlet poppies. To the rhythm of the barrage, the Searcher stamps out her agonizing dance of life and death, symbolizing the ancient sacrifice of all mothers and daughters in war.

Now that scene is lost in darkness and the barrage becomes the lonely voices of wounded men howling with abandon over an old motion picture show as the cinema hut becomes melo-dramatically alive, with the Searcher guiding her helpless charges.

Swiftly the ramp stage contracts into a dazzling white tube wide enough to hold eight horses or forty men.* The ambulance train is walled with two tiers of white bunks occupied by bandaged soldiers. The Searcher works her way up and down the grateful alley of wounded, dispensing aid and comfort. She is about to offer a cup to a wounded enemy. "No, Miss Red Cross! It's against all orders," shouts the Officer. "Don't." The scene stands still. The Searcher obeys, and in dismay drops her tray. The train stops dead. She stumbles out and disappears hissing to herself, "Shame . . . shame."

The stage irises open as silver train tracks dance into sight and crisscross and multiply into crosses lost in the stars. The ramp becomes alive with hundreds of silver crosses. The starlit night grows radiant over the garden of graves on Honeymoon Hill. A great milky moon shapes itself beyond the crimson hill and bathes the Searcher crouching between two mounds at the front of the ramp. Like a sibyl she pours forth from her agony her prophecy of the eternal waste and the destruction of war to all the young dead beneath her and to the surviving audience in this theatre of war. Then comes an earthshaking crash. The heavens are a holocaust. Cleansing crimson flames sweep the hill and obliterate the stars. The outcry of an army of anguished voices is heard dying down, extinguishing itself, expiring. The clean moon and the host of stars reappear in ordered array. Healing light sifts down over the graves, silent save for a humming psalm of peaceful jubilation heard beneath the chant of the Searcher, who, her mission accomplished, surrenders herself unto death as "Taps" far away rings out its frugal notes.

* The boxcars of French troop trains during the First World War were marked, "Forty men or eight horses." — Ed.

The Searcher, The hospital

The Searcher, "Mess Hut . . ."

Girl Crazy, Curtain

Girl Crazy

by Guy Bolton and John McGowan

Music and lyrics by George and Ira Gershwin
Produced by Alex A. Aarons and Vinton Freedley
With Ethel Merman, Ginger Rogers, and Willie Howard
Alvin Theatre, 1930

In 1930, 233 new productions opened in 70 theatres all crowded within the area of 16 blocks along Broadway. *Girl Crazy* opened against three other productions, including Jane Cowl in *Twelfth Night* and the Dietz and Schwartz revue, *Three's a Crowd.*

For many reasons, including the fabulous Gershwin score, this new musical comedy was a prestissimo show. Without billing, a little bundle of fire by the name of Ethel Merman became overnight the first lady of the American musical theatre with her tricky and defiant rhythms that rose in brassy crescendo with "Sam and Delilah" and "I Got Rhythm." Ginger Rogers surfaced to stardom with "Embraceable You" and a brief dance on the broad brim of a Mexican sombrero. Veteran Willie Howard was at his burlesque best, and young Benny Goodman was blowing his way up in the orchestra.

In this boy-meets-girl show, a "girl crazy" playboy is dispatched by his father in a taxi from New York to a cattle ranch out West to remove him from the perils of the night clubs. He converts the ranch into a dude resort, imports his old cronies (thirty-two ladies and gentlemen of the ensemble) from the Great White Way, and finally marries the local post-mistress. When Vinton Freedley described the locale of *Girl Crazy* I was enchanted. The scene was Custerville, a ram-shackle cattle town in the Arizona desert. I had already explored the mountains and deserts of the Southwest, and the art of the Pueblo Indians fascinated me. How to contain all this on the stage of his Alvin Theatre?

In the twenties, most musicals had a show curtain framed with an appropriate portal which gave the musical visual style and provided for alternating scenes "in one." The vogue of changing scenery in view of the audience had not yet arrived. For my first musical, *Good News,* I had designed the portal and curtain to orient the campus of Tait College for the audience. *The New Moon* had a rococo portal that framed the traveler with the frigate *New Moon* docked in eighteenth century New Orleans. *Heads Up* had an Art Deco portal and curtain of sand, sea, and sky for a beach resort.

This is the Custerville show curtain and portal I concocted for *Girl Crazy.* The portal's abstract pattern in charcoal, sepia, and old white was derived from designs of ancient Mimbres pottery. These bold, neutral portals framed cactus and sagebrush, alkali desert and buttes, the hotel and post office of Custerville, as well as a chic Mexican resort. Vinton Freedley, a producer of impeccable taste, blanched when I confided I would like to paint all these scenes in an arbitrary palette of vermilion, purple, yellow, and juniper green, with saddle brown and white adobe against pointilliste skies of yellow and cerulean blue. That was when I discovered he was color-blind! Only when I explained we would introduce to the contemporary musical stage the brilliant intensities of the Southwest, as well as the local color of *Girl Crazy*'s giddy shenanigans, was his faith in my sense of color restored.

After the opening, one critic, also obviously color-blind, confessed, "They could lay the scene in the Gobi Desert and still the show would be a smash hit!"

The Emperor Jones

by Eugene O'Neill

Directed by George Pierce Baker
Yale School of Drama, 1931

George Pierce Baker recognized Eugene O'Neill's talent for playwriting at Harvard. He always encouraged him and gave him hope for success. In 1925 Baker left Harvard and founded the Yale School of Drama. The following year, in recognizing the art of the theatre, Yale awarded his former student an honorary degree. Baker wrote to O'Neill urging him "to let nothing stand in the way of being here to receive the degree. When it is given to you next June it means to me, not only the honor to you but the establishment of this fact: hereafter a man writing on the subject of his choice as his mind urges him to write, will still meet with misunderstanding and doubt but there will be the precedent established that institutions of learning in this country should recognize him if his honesty of purpose results in genuinely significant accomplishment. . . . It is another milepost."

In 1931 Baker wanted to present the first performance of O'Neill's *Lazarus Laughed,* utilizing all the resources of the Yale Drama School. Matters beyond his control intervened. Instead, he staged a new production of O'Neill's challenging tour de force, *The Emperor Jones*. Written in a new technique of swiftly moving episodes, *The Emperor Jones* depicts the inner disintegration of a one-time Pullman porter and traces his reversion from the outer order of social convention to the primitive superstitions of his black ancestors. Jones has become the swaggering, self-made emperor of one of the islands of the West Indies. The natives are rising up against his greedy tyranny. The monotonous drumming of their pursuit casts its spell over Jones. Confident of the protective power of his silver bullet, Jones dives into the jungle to cross the island and escape to safety on a passing vessel. Six of the play's eight scenes are a monologue beginning in late afternoon and ending on the close of night.

O'Neill was always verbally explicit and visually sensitive about his settings. His explanatory crude line drawings for the scenes of *The Emperor Jones* reveal his understanding of design and the significance of setting as symbolic background for dramatic action.

In designing *The Emperor Jones* I felt the jungle must reflect those visible and tangible shapes conjured up by Jones's dark fears. The jungle thus became a participant in the play, a terrible presence from which Jones must escape. The events of his flight occurred around a low mound in the center of the stage like the altar in a Greek theatre or the ritualistic dancing place of some remote jungle tribe. There was no scenery in the real sense, only the potent magic of changing light. The scenes faded into one another like fragments of restless dreams. One scene would lose its focus and disappear in the sharpening outlines of a succeeding one. The lighting was brilliantly realized with the collaboration of my colleague Stanley McCandless by means of projections on a cyclorama hung with folds of dark gauze for added texture and depth.

The forest that Jones first enters is impenetrable, as O'Neill suggests, "like a wall of darkness dividing the world" of Jones-the-white-man-by-day and Jones-the-black-man-by-night. In his hallucinations the realistic tree forms of the jungle become the habitation of dark, brooding spirits. There is a clear affinity between nature's rhythmic shapes and forms found in bursting buds, the structure of plants, uprearing tree trunks, and the plastic shapes and forms of African sculpture. By means of light projections I visually dramatized this symbolic relationship, believing with Thornton Wilder that "the theatre longs to represent the symbol of things, not the things themselves. When the theatre pretends to give the real thing in canvas and wood and metal it loses something of the realer thing which is its true business." Progressing from scene to scene, nature's tree forms increasingly assume the characteristics of black primitive sculpture.

In the convict scene the tree trunks, solemn like prison bars, resemble towering rude posts. In the slave market those posts assume the form of totem poles, surveying the phantom crowd of slave merchants pressing around Jones's body, erect on the auction block. In the slave ship bound for America, the totems of the previous scene meld into monstrous Negro fetishes cradling two rows of ebony bodies. Spotlights from below cast their distorted shadows among the fetishes. These turbulent shadows absorb Jones's frenzied body.

In the climactic scene, Jones comes upon a ghostly Congo Witch Doctor, "stained all over a bright red," gyrating in a ritual around "a rough structure of boulders" beneath a huge tree; or rather, it may once have been a tree, for now the voodoo altar is dwarfed beneath the widespread crotch of a giant fetish. With the crashing finale of the tomtoms, Jones, stripped of the conventional veneer of civilization, stands before this magic apparition who bids him sacrifice himself to his own primitive heritage. But Jones rejects it and commits himself to what O'Neill was ever acutely conscious of — "the one eternal tragedy of Man in his glorious self-destructive struggle." Ironically, the white man's silver bullet fails to save Jones from his imagined illusions, and he is destroyed by the natives.

That grotesque scene vanishes with the first light of dawn, and a mist shrouds the dark wall of the forest. Through the night, Jones had made a futile circle through the forest. A Cockney trader gloats mockingly over his lifeless body: "Where's yer 'igh an' mighty airs now, yer bloomin' Majesty? [Then with a grin] Silver bullets. Gawd blimey, but yer died in the 'eight o' style, any'ow!"

Like the dying shadow of Jones's lost empire, the wall of the forest vanishes into the beach and the sea, and on the horizon rest cumulus clouds — eerie and incredible, like the mirage of Jones's incredible dream.

The Emperor Jones, Slave ship

44

The Emperor Jones, Giant fetish

The Flying Dutchman

by Richard Wagner

A Project, 1932

Wagner derived his romantic text for *The Flying Dutchman* from Heine's legend of the sea captain who, having vainly tried to pass the Cape of Good Hope, was condemned for his blasphemy to sail the oceans forever on a phantom ship with a phantom crew. Wagner improved on the legend by adding a twist of love. Once in seven years the Dutchman might go ashore to seek a woman who would be faithful to him until death, and only then would he be released from the ancient curse of the sea.

The designer must have instinctive rapport for the weight and the volume of Wagner's music for *The Flying Dutchman*. His designs derive from the musical ideas of the characters rather than from the characters themselves, and also from the particular events of Wagner's libretto which he considered only the framework for his music. The designer translates music into the visual — sometimes symbolic — scenic media of the stage, so that his scenes come to look like the sound of music. Wagner's music is far from realistic. Then why realistic scenery? De-emphasize truth to nature. In the process, elements of nature are exaggerated in the direction of truth to become meaningful symbols. The very word "operatic" implies this heightened sense of exaggeration.

All great operas, like *Fidelio, Otello,* and *The Flying Dutchman,* deal with larger-than-life matters. They do not flourish under naturalistic projection. At its best, opera is an interpretive art of high stylization. Singing and recitative are not normal means of communication as speech and pantomime are normal in the theatre. In the "Liebestod" great voices take over and elevate us when words fail. This vocal phenomenon of human expression is at the core of the art of opera and defines the artistic limitations and the conventions of the operatic style.

The Flying Dutchman is set along the rugged seacoast of Norway with its moods changing beneath changing skies. The sea and the ships that sail that sea, both Daland's ship and the eerie Flying Dutchman's, play significant roles in the opera's score. They are pictorial motives rendered into ever present symbols that may assume multiple meanings for the audience. This makes the spectator an active participant who identifies personally with these diverse symbols.

During the first act, Daland's ship is driven ashore after a long voyage in a raging storm. Very soon, out of the darkness, the pale negative shadow of the phantom ship with its spectral crew looms up alongside. Both anchor in the inky waters of the rocky shore — one freestanding in light, the other condemned to cast no shadow. The Dutchman, after his appointed cycle of wandering over the seven seas, seeks shelter with Daland, whom he would make rich in order to marry his daughter, Senta, already betrothed to Erik.

The third act shows the harbor with Daland's ship docked beside his house. His crew celebrate their safe return and Senta's approaching wedding. Close by, the shadowless phantom ship is cradled in a bony, barren dock. High up on this dock appears the Dutchman out of the darkness, gazing down on Senta with Erik. He overhears Erik: "Has this stranger bewitched you?" The Dutchman, discovering his love for Senta is unrequited, calls down to her, "All is lost. You have shattered my hopes for peace forever." "My love is true," she proclaims, highly agitated, "I will save you yet." Condemned to the sea once more, he boards his ghostly ship, prepares to sail, and vanishes out over the watery plain free of wind and tide. Senta, consumed with exaltation, breaks free from her father, Erik, and the crowd, and rushes to the top of the reeling stairs of the deserted dock. "I am faithful unto death!" she cries out, and throws herself into the embracing sea. Above the horizon, with Wagner's theme of Redemption rising to a serene orchestral cadence, ascend two enveloping cloud forms. At such a supreme moment one shares with Schiller his belief that "when music reaches its noblest power, it becomes form in space." These cloud forms are seen to draw up the waters of the sea into the sky, and are finally joined together in space — symbolizing the dissolution of the legendary curse of the Flying Dutchman through the consuming love of Senta.

The Flying Dutchman, Harbor, arrival of the Dutchman

The Flying Dutchman, Finale

The Lady from the Sea

by Henrik Ibsen

Produced by Nathan Zatkin
Directed by John Houseman
Little Theatre, 1934

In 1923 Duse moved huge audiences in the Metropolitan Opera House with her incandescent interpretation of *The Lady from the Sea,* though some critics felt Ibsen's drama was a tedious and nebulous work.

In the thirties it was still feasible for a dedicated group to undertake a revival on Broadway of this semi-symbolic classic on a budget that was no more than Duse's salary for one week. John Houseman, who had just had his first success directing *Four Saints in Three Acts,* approached the play with intelligence and a sense of style. If we did not entirely succeed in bringing forth a unified, realistic concept of Ibsen's notoriously difficult symbolism onto our raked platforms and atmospheric backdrops, the production was fresh, adroit, and we thought full of grace.

Stark Young, a critic ever intuitive and responsive to the visual theatre, felt our settings for *The Lady from the Sea* "were carried through with great simplicity of means and with a curiously dramatic instinct to the play's demands. The garden scene, with the distant mountains and the near rushes of the pool, was a revelation of what out-of-doors may be." Brooks Atkinson lamented that "the inadequacy of the current revival becomes all the more apparent before Donald

Oenslager's settings — in fact, the play might be acted forcefully by a simple exhibition of Mr. Oenslager's settings. They are the quintessence of dramatic poetry." But I hasten to respond that a simple exhibition of settings is scarcely a substitute for a living performance in the theatre. I would prefer Duse.

In his vivid memoir, *Run-Through* (1972), John Houseman recalled that in *The Lady from the Sea* "Donald Oenslager did so well that he stole the show." That is flattering, but I have always told my students that settings that are applauded or steal the show are perhaps impressive but unsuccessful, for they detract from the play. When designer, director, and actors collaborate so that the play steals the show, that is theatre as it should be.

Ibsen had the poet's instinct and the artist's impulse for the mountains and the sea. The settings for *The Lady from the Sea* were brief indications of places set against the poetic atmosphere of stormy fiords, mountains, clouds, and hilltops. I share Brooks Atkinson's observation that creating the illusion of the broad out-of-doors behind a proscenium requires a special art. Few designers today achieve it — not simply the illusion, but the flow and lift of the out-of-doors. The grace of nature is at the beginning and the end of everything on earth. Any art that leaves nature out leaves the life of man partially unexplored. And that is what the theatre has always been about. The theatre cannot escape it in any long view of life. A five-year-old child, growing restless during the garden scene of the Moscow Art Theatre's *The Seagull,* whispered, "Mother, let's go into the garden there for a walk." For that child, admittedly, the scenery stole the show. He was enchanted by the illusion of nature which he saw on the stage. To strike responsive chords in the audience, to enchant, to transport that audience into another world — that, not applause, is the designer's real reward in the theatre.

The Lady from the Sea, Garden

Dance with your Gods

by Kenneth Perkins

Produced by Laurence Schwab
Directed by Robert Sinclair
Mansfield Theatre, 1934

In the theatre every new production becomes a conspiracy. With Kenneth Perkins' *Dance with your Gods*, producer Laurence Schwab was the impetuous ringleader, confident his play had the same potential for artistic and financial success as *Macbeth*. Director Robert Sinclair, myself as designer, and a cast of fine actors enthusiastically read themselves into the new script — recognizing its tantalizing possibilities as a vehicle for the exercise of our talents. The locale of *Dance with your Gods* was old New Orleans. The scenes were laden with picturesque and moody atmosphere: a sultry Creole mansion, haunting scenes up alleyways of shantytown, a voodoo meeting among bales of cotton in a shadowy warehouse.

As involvements in production details increased, mounting enthusiasm was generated for the production. During strenuous weeks of rehearsal, everyone, including the author, easily lost his perspective about the play. Through the climactic dress rehearsals, with voodoo drums reverberating through the theatre, the company observed their play come to dramatic life. Then came the trial of opening night with hopes for success high. The next day *Dance with your Gods* received a hopeless set of disillusioning reviews — "a trifle which failed to translate the theme of voodooism into the black magic of a play." Laurence Schwab had no alternative but to post the closing notice. In due course trucks arrived to cart off the defunct scenery of old New Orleans for dissection in Cain's warehouse or to be burned on a funeral pyre on the Jersey flats. Perhaps in the late afternoon that day, looking west from Times Square, one saw not the setting sun but a glorious blaze of "fireproofed" scenery lighting up the sky.

Prestigious direction, notable acting, and an eye-filling production can contribute to the success of a play, but they cannot rescue the play from its own shortcomings. Everything crashes into memory with the failure of the play. But the theatre has a determined way of accepting failure and rising above it; and, like an echo, a new production becomes once again another exciting conspiracy in the theatre.

Dance with your Gods, Shantytown

Tristan and Isolde

by Richard Wagner

Presented by the Philadelphia Orchestra
Directed by Herbert Graf
Conducted by Fritz Reiner
The Academy of Music, 1934

Tristan and Isolde opened the Philadelphia Orchestra's ambitious 1934–1935 opera season in the Academy of Music, with Fritz Reiner conducting the first uncut production of the opera in this country. Herbert Graf, the Austrian avant-garde stage director, escaping from Nazi persecution, made his American debut. The artist Archipenko had been commissioned to design the scenes. Apparently his sculptured models were "fascinating but hardly practical."

Musical wavelengths reported that for some time I had been evolving ideas for a modern solution to the design problems of Tristan's score through a synthesis of movement, light, and setting. A hurried phone call, and I was on the train to Philadelphia, armed with a few assertive sketches to confer with Graf. The Herr Doktor Professor was blessed with Viennese humor and a limited English vocabulary. His comments on our warm hotel room, our lighting system, or the state of our theatrical unions began or ended with: "It is not to believe." However, we soon discovered we saw eye to eye on Tristan and Isolde. We shared a mutual admiration for the great Appia and his imaginative approach to and perceptive analysis of Wagner's music-drama. So we agreed to collaborate on this most important task.

On September 18 he wrote from Philadelphia: "Excuse my words. But: I have refused the models of Archipenko and therefore I have on the other side the great responsibility, that we bring in a better way also a *perfectly new event*. All artists and critics in New York and here are awaiting from us for the *new* opera style in Amerika, *no compromise*. . . . Regarding *Tristan* it means: *the new* visionary—Light—*Tristan,* as in your first sketches."

My preliminary designs for *Tristan* were for a long-range project whose completion required much more thought and further exploration, but unfortunately now they had to be realized on very short notice and under high pressure. The final designs, and the building and painting of the scenes, had to be completed in four weeks — weeks which for me were also filled with the scenic responsibilities for five other productions opening at the same time.

Tristan and Isolde is a drama of surpassing grandeur between a man and a woman who dream and live on their own secret fires of unquenchable love. Through the opera runs the conflict between the outer world and the inner world of Tristan and Isolde — reality versus pure spirit — Day against Night. They dream of escaping from the restless world of day "into that night of the inner world of the spirit in which their souls become one." Their world of the spirit finds consummation in the potion scene on Tristan's ship, in the "Liebestod" of the last act. All their other scenes are encounters in the tragic world of reality and light.

For Graf and me, the settings should interpret this dualism of Day and Night. Ship's rigging, artificial flowers, and painted masonry are earthbound relics of outworn tradition. The settings are timeless. Let the scenes be bounded by high folds of transparent gauze. As each act begins, the gauze curtains open to reveal some actual indication of scene. Always present through the gauze is a hint of the sea, whose surface is the world of illusion over which the lovers pass. In the beginning of the first act the leitmotif of the sea appears in the song of the sailor. The sea assumes as many transformations in mood as does the motif with the orchestra. Thus, the enclosing gauze and the sea also dramatize the conflict of Night and Day.

Tristan's ship is like no ship that has ever sailed the seas. Its reality is no more than a great taut sail and two flights of stairs that sweep up to the heroic and ancient prow. Pendant folds of gauze suggest the sweep of sails bellying over water. All is blue and old-white — blue as the Irish sea whence the ship has come. There is no sunlight, for Isolde's thoughts are of her loveless future, and the sea is dark and land is near. When Isolde bids Brangaene seek out Tristan, Brangaene does not traditionally hoist a great lifeless sail to reveal Tristan. As she ascends the stairs, lights behind the sail, opaque until now, reveal Tristan and Kurvenal surrounded by their crew. And later, while Isolde ponders the time she saved and nursed Tristan, the motif of "Tristan Wounded" is heard, and through the pale transparency of the sail, Tristan appears at the helm of their ship as though in her imagination.

Now the ship approaches Cornwall. The lights darken, and they will grow darker still through the potion scene. From the moment the lovers turn from death to love, warm light suffuses them. The great sail overhead fades into a gray Cornish sky and King Mark's castle appears as a shadow of itself. There is no longer any sea, and Tristan and Isolde are one in their own world. Of a sudden, Mark's envoys board and bedeck the ship. All is bathed in radiant light. The music is fortissimo, C major — trumpets. The crew rejoices. The voyage is over.

Our interpretation of *Tristan and Isolde* went far beyond the traditional tastes and sensibilities of American audiences in the early thirties. Many of our lighting effects, devised to enhance the mood of the score, surprised and shocked the audience. The critical reception was divided — violently pro and con. Lawrence Gilman of the *Herald Tribune* described our unorthodox conception as "staggeringly heretical" and the "beginning of a new era in opera." Olin Downes of *The Times* found our innovative ideas "a thousand miles from the romanticism and spaciousness of Wagner's work."

From Valhalla that evening Wagner must have been peering down bemused by the spontaneous combustion *Tristan and Isolde* set off in the City of Brotherly Love. Wagner was preeminently a man of the theatre. If any composer-producer lived on the stimulation of change in his time, it was Wagner. We in our time set out to release his opera from the encrusted formulas and cumulative conventions of the Bayreuth traditions. Since then, much has been achieved in our opera houses across our country to advance the changing conceptions of Wagnerian *mis-en-scène*.

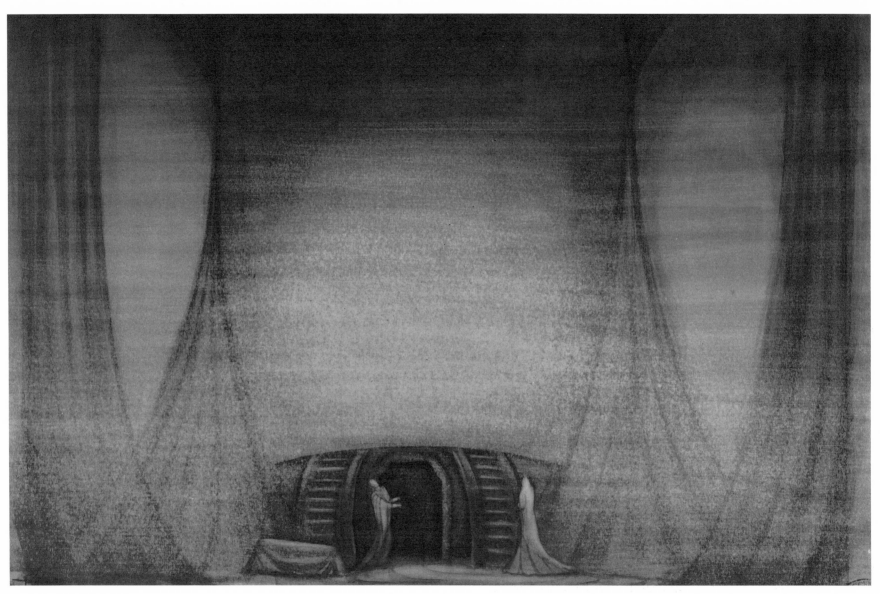

Tristan and Isolde, Ship

Tristan and Isolde, Finale

Anything Goes

by Howard Lindsay and Russell Crouse

Music and lyrics by Cole Porter
Directed by Howard Lindsay
Produced by Vinton Freedley
Alvin Theatre, 1934

In 1934 Vinton Freedley was on vacation fishing near the Pearl Islands in the Pacific when he conceived the idea of a Caribbean cruise for a musical, to be called *Anything Goes*. He returned home and signed up those three peerless entertainers, Ethel Merman, William Gaxton, and Victor Moore. While cruising down the Rhine, Cole Porter invented one of his most sophisticated albums of music with dashing, impudent lyrics. The book was entrusted to those literate London humorists, Guy Bolton and P. G. Wodehouse. Their script was just finished when the *Morro Castle* burned and sank, and with it all the humor of their book. Howard Lindsay, directing the show, and Russel Crouse salvaged and converted the original book into the lively adventures of some zany passengers on a transatlantic luxury liner.

The production went into rehearsal with the script far from finished. Most of the scenes would take place on the lido afterdeck, the main lounge, sundry staterooms, and even the brig of the liner. My streamlined ship, anchored to a revolving stage to facilitate scene changes, was fitted out in the sawdust atmosphere of the scene shop of Bernie McDonald, Broadway's master craftsman-technician in the twenties and thirties. While this ship could never sail the seas with the speed of the *Bremen* or the *Rex,* she incorporated all the newest trends of maritime design. Her three white decks with sleek brass fittings and her streamlined funnel dominated a white sky above a cobalt sea.

The production schedule of *Anything Goes* was sailing ahead; but even the producer did not know how or where his show would end. Friday, before the Boston opening, a desperate SOS call to the harassed authors: "Where does our finale take place?" "We aren't sure yet, Don! Just give us a scene in London where everybody can get married — indoors or out." I recalled an enlightening conversation with Lee Strasberg describing his impression of a certain scene as "an interior with an exterior feeling." *There* was the final scene for *Anything Goes*. Within three days, a trellised "interior-exterior" was designed, built, and with the paint still wet, sent to Boston just in time for the opening. The program called the scene "The Conservatory of Sir Eveleyn's home in England" — just the place for the cast of *Anything Goes* to end up for a long run.

While never a good sailor, in the theatre I often had to go to sea with scripts demanding tricky nautical know-how. One tramp steamer burned up nightly sailing through the Marianas. A freighter exploded and sank at sea. Another rose in the Pedro Miguel locks and proceeded through the Panama Canal. In 1934, four of the eleven productions I designed included water craft: Tristan's ship for the Philadelphia Orchestra; several Erie Canal boats for Marc Connelly's *The Farmer Takes a Wife;* for *Gold Eagle Guy* a clipper ship beached in San Francisco; and the transatlantic liner for *Anything Goes*. For six hectic weeks of overlapping production schedules I was ubiquitous, commuting between theatres in New York, Philadelphia, and Boston, launching all those unsinkable "painted ships upon a painted ocean."

Anything Goes, Ship's deck

Tapestry in Gray

by Martin Flavin

Directed by Marion Gering
Produced by B. P. Shulberg
Shubert Theatre, 1935

To the wonder of most Broadway designers, elaborate scenic investiture was a recognized factor in attracting the patronage of playgoers in the latter half of the thirties. Plenty of money was available and managers were not afraid to spend it. And for the rival producer from the West Coast, there was always the possibility of converting a Broadway production into a viable Hollywood picture.

B. P. Shulberg, former production head of Paramount Pictures, decided to produce Martin Flavin's *Tapestry in Gray* on Broadway. It was a play in thirty-seven scenes that tried hard to be a motion picture even before it could be filmed. Marion Gering arrived from Hollywood to "conceive and stage" the production. He was a Russian who had once worked with Meierhold in Moscow, became active as a director on Broadway, and later was sunkist with Hollywood success.

The play was new to the theatre in theme and form. After studying the script, I envisioned the design for *Tapestry in Gray* on very simple lines. Instead of filling the stage with all the realistic trappings known to Broadway, why not do the play in one large room with the spontaneity of a charade? Several horizontal levels would provide a variety of acting areas. Only properties essential to the action would suggest a hotel, a hospital, or a bistro, and enable the play to move with alacrity over land and sea. The producer objected to my simplistic concept, insisting on a "Hollywood style" show. Against my better judgment, Mr. Gering persuaded me to devise a neoplastic, environmental arrangement of skyscrapers, something like a Mondrian View with a Room, through whose cubistic cubbyholes Mr. Flavin's intimate vignettes could hop-skip-and-jump and with mobile light meld into each other like fade-outs and fade-ins.

The stage of the Shubert Theatre was filled with gray velour scenery that rose forty-five feet into the grid and spilled out into the orchestra pit. While the scenery was being set up, Lee Shubert made his way onto the stage strewn with more electric cable and spotlights than he had ever seen and confidentially asked Edward Kook, president of Century Lighting, "Do we need so much equipment to make it dark?" Mr. Kook hinted cryptically that the dark is never light enough.

One of the nicer episodes of that ill-fated production centered on two baroque lanterns that had always flanked the proscenium of the Shubert Theatre; one was referred to as Mr. Lee, the other as J. J. Those house lanterns interfered seriously with the lighting and extended sightlines of *Tapestry*'s settings. Permission was reluctantly granted to remove "Mr. Lee" and "J. J." from their own house.

Tapestry in Gray was one of those plays designed to prove that the theatre lacks the flexibility of screen expression. As the designer, I had to do a cinematic job which no stage designer should be asked to do in the theatre. While my setting was only as elaborate as the author's writing demanded, the production inflated his modest play into such a grandiose effigy on Broadway that it never reached the cameras in Hollywood.

Tapestry in Gray, Stage set

Ten Million Ghosts

by Sidney Kingsley

Produced and directed by Mr. Kingsley
St. James Theatre, 1936

In his third play, *Ten Million Ghosts,* Sidney Kingsley discharged a broadside of accusation and indignation against the international munitions cartels that had profited from the First World War. This kaleidoscopic piece was not so much a play as a dramatic lecture employing a mixed-media presentation and requiring ten elaborate realistic scenes to provide pictorial support and visual expression.

Mr. Kingsley produced his epic with insistent realism and largesse. He was indefatigable and expected complete and selfless cooperation from all who worked with him — designers, actors, and crew. Final rehearsals were all-night affairs, interrupted at midnight by a procession of waiters from Sardi's with trays of food for the hungry. The weary crews on the cramped stage of the St. James Theatre groaned with the physical burden of it all. Two eighteen-foot revolving stages kept the complicated palatial interiors, noble offices, even a hotel ballroom, in ordered motion. A thirty-foot Quonset hut flew and folded in mid -air for storage.

The play's prologue was a scenic description of a vast gunworks in full operation. As the designer, I was invited to shoot the works. This can be very risky. John Anderson, the critic, felt that scene for the prologue was "more valid and eloquent than anything else in the play, with its lazy gray monsters turning slowly over in their sleek rhythm, their flanks smoothed by solicitous workers amid the screech and whine of steel on steel, the dim prelude to the noise they must inevitably make to split, not the ears, but the world." As director, Sidney Kingsley was a meticulous artist about every detail of the production. Upstage in the middle distance one worker was hoisted aloft on a finished cannon. That actor was a midget engaged to complete the scene's optical illusion of the setting's perspective! John Anderson inquires, "What can a playwright say to hold the stage in the midst of scenery like that unless he speaks with deep power and persuasion, unless, in fact he can silence the monsters by his very words? . . . The playwright must be quite certain that a play's values will not be dwarfed by the proportions of his production." Sidney Kingsley had depended on the accuracy of his production to complete his writing for him.

On opening night the ghosts of those merchants of death had their ironic revenge. The house curtain stuck halfway up to its high trim and revealed only half of the Universe Forges. Thereafter the curtain never failed until it was finally rung down when *Ten Million Ghosts* closed after eleven performances. What happened to all those settings? Producers must pay to have them destroyed. Occasionally part of a set may go astray. One day, long after *Ten Million Ghosts* had closed, I ran across my gun lathe of the Universe Forges. It had miraculously found its way to a vacant lot on the West Side, where it had become a peaceable jungle gym for all the neighborhood kids. *Sic transit gloria scenarum!*

Ten Million Ghosts, Munitions factory

Sweet River

by George Abbott

Directed and Produced by Mr. Abbott
Fifty-first Street Theatre, 1936

Uncle Tom's Cabin appealed to George Abbott ever since he saw the barnstorming "Tom" shows in his youth. When he first thought of doing a modern version of his favorite classic, he had in mind a free adaptation of Harriet Beecher Stowe's novel published in 1851. The result was *Sweet River,* a sentimental excursion into the theatrical past with authentic scenes and costumes to re-create the atmosphere of the Old South. Abbott brought unhackneyed showmanship, humanity, and unstinted affection to his Broadway canvas of the antebellum South. The Juanita Hall Singers bridged the scenes with spirituals, and much of the action was accompanied by choral singing. This was a "Tom" show for a new era — without blackface, without traditional scenery, without Lawyer Marks, without Little Eva's death scene, without even the apotheosis.

Three years before, I had designed the Players' Club revival of this American classic with an all-star cast. Otis Skinner played Uncle Tom. It was presented with full respect for the play's time-honored traditions. The twenty-five scenes moved swiftly to free the stage for the actors. The settings frankly relied on theatrical artifice — painted perspective to record the scenic artist's taste of the fifties. Only "practical" properties were real. For the rest, the painter's imagination played over canvas drops and wings and profiles. Chairs, portraits, curtains, flowers, and fountains were painted realities.

But *Sweet River* called for the modern style. It was financed by Warner Brothers, who saw in George Abbott's play the possibility of a great American folk film. They converted their Broadway cinema palace, the Hollywood Theatre, into a legitimate theatre and planned its opening with *Sweet River.* The largest turntable in New York (forty-five feet in diameter) was installed to expedite the stage effects and scene changes.

Through the prologue drop appeared a canopied avenue of live oaks and Spanish moss, sheltering the whitewashed cabins of St. Clair's slave quarters that stretched lazily away to distant sunny cotton fields. They contrasted with the airy lilac drawing room of St. Clair's plantation house. Later, Eliza, seeking refuge from Simon Legree in a rude tavern, escaped with her baby through a window. Pursued by bloodhounds, she actually dashed from the snowbound shore over the moving ice floes which diminished in the distance as the revolving stage carried her over the black Ohio to the opposite shore and safety. The dramatic auction mart for slaves was a chiaroscuro study in washes of brown and black and old white. *Sweet River* was a scene designer's idyll.

George Abbott reverently and profligately wasted both skill and beauty on Mrs. Stowe's old melodrama that cried out to be played melodramatically. The audience hissed and applauded as if they were at a spoof revival of a "Tom" show, which was the last thing in the world that *Sweet River* aimed at being. If only the audience could have gone to this play forgetting it was *Uncle Tom's Cabin,* they would have had a very good time. But they could not see it on its own merits. It had been George Abbott's dream to do right by his old stage favorite, but after five performances *Sweet River* faded into nostalgic memory.

Anything Goes, Ship's deck

Red, Hot and Blue!

by Howard Lindsay and Russel Crouse

Music and Lyrics by Cole Porter
Directed by Howard Lindsay
Dances and Ensembles by George Hale
Produced by Vinton Freedley
Alvin Theatre, 1936

The theatre for me has always been far-ranging and its art timeless. As a designer I have been interested as much in why things were done as in how they were done. The past is always present. Old life flows into the new; new uses appear for the old. The unchanging stuff of past experience can be made to fit into the latest idiom. Thus the theatre of each generation finds renewed expression in flexible experiment.

In the thirties I became absorbed in the modern application of the time-honored theatrical traditions of perspective. I employed various principles of perspective in designing *Uncle Tom's Cabin, Johnny Johnson, Sweet River,* and *Ten Million Ghosts.* For a long time I nursed a plan to design an entire production, preferably a contemporary musical show, in which modern decor would be superimposed on the traditional style of painted perspective.

In the fall of 1936 along came Vinton Freedley with his ideas for *Red, Hot and Blue.* He always worked on the principle of the tailor-made musical comedy. He engaged the same team who had made *Anything Goes* a hit two seasons before. Howard Lindsay and Russel Crouse would write the book. Cole Porter would come from Hollywood to fashion the lyrics and music for Jimmy Durante, Bob Hope, and Ethel Merman, whom he had already engaged. George Hale would attend to the dances and ensembles. Constance Ripley would design the clothes. I would devise settings that should move swiftly from a penthouse in New York to many Washington landmarks — Pennsylvania Avenue, the Dolly Madison House, the Capitol, the White House and its South Lawn. I succeeded in persuading Freedley and director Howard Lindsay to let me give a fresh pictorial style to the show by frankly painting all the scenery in perspective. They confessed they showed great courage in accepting my ideas and then left me to my noble experiment.

Little did I realize the difficulties that lay ahead in translating my designs into painted perspective. I soon learned that to achieve the illusion of three-dimensional objects with flat scenery called for three times as much effort as the accepted methods of stage design. In converting my perspective designs into scale models I discovered the conflict of the "variable" scale of scenery arranged in true perspective and the "invariable" scale of the actor moving up and down stage within that scenery. Also, I learned that perspective drawing of a scene could not be accurately preserved when transferred to the wing and border system. When it became clear that true perspective would not work, my assistant Isaac Benesch and I became red, hot, and blue all over! I sought the help of a consultant, Robert de Postels, a mathematician and an expert on optics who fortunately loved the theatre.

Red, Hot and Blue employed all the old tight tricks of perspective, but they were concealed beneath loose brushwork and flowing vivid color. Ethel Merman's swank penthouse was a Venetian drawing room in copper tones adorned with Tiepolo frescoes, glass chandelier and sconces, Venetian furniture, and orchidaceous flower arrangements all stylishly painted on profile wings and borders.

The show curtain was an isometric perspective projection of the National Capitol. A front drop with a view up Pennsylvania Avenue toward the Capitol was freely rendered in one-point perspective. Dolly Madison's bedroom, with all the original furnishings including her four-poster bed, was reduced by the painter's skill to profiled make-believe. The finale on the

South Lawn of the White House was achieved with three foliage leg drops framing the columned Rotunda, all loosely painted over precise drawing.

Of course it could be made to work. Perspective had worked in the theatre for two hundred years. We found that the perspective treatises of the great Baroque scenographers, Andrea Pozzo and Ferdinando Bibiena, were of immediate assistance. Based on a formula involving projected sight lines and plane geometry, our problem was conveniently solved by establishing progressive vanishing points for each wing and border as they receded upstage.

The next hurdle was the execution of the scenery. My builders' drawings and painters' elevations contained all the detailed perspective instructions. The complicated scenic production required the combined efforts of two major studios. The Triangle Scenery Studio took on the exterior scenes, which were executed on the floor. Theirs was the traditional continental system of scene painting. The Robert W. Bergman Studio executed the interior scenes on paint frames that were raised and lowered through slots on the paint bridge. This was the accepted American system of scene painting, but it did not facilitate the perspective problems of the scenic artists. Drawing the full-scale perspective lines necessitated securing the cord to a vanishing point on the lower floor of the scenic studio and stretching the cord up through the slot of the third-floor paint bridge to the surface of the canvas on the paint frame. Painting scenery in perspective requires mechanical accuracy in line drawing. It cannot be left to the scenic artist's eye.

Today only a few old-timers in a few scenic studios can lay out a complicated drop drawn in two- or three-point perspective. It is almost a lost art because in our current disjointed theatre real perspective is rarely called for. Yet the convention of painted scenery has a legitimate place on our stage because of its very artifice. The freedom, economy, and craftsmanship of painted scenery open unlimited possibilities for those with the eye to rediscover the vanishing point of perspective and to explore new directions for its practical and aesthetic use in today's changing theatre.

Red, Hot and Blue!, White House

Johnny Johnson

by Paul Green and Kurt Weill

Music by Kurt Weill
Directed by Lee Strasberg
Produced by the Group Theatre
Forty-Fourth Street Theatre, 1936

During the summer of 1936, the Group Theatre provided entertainment for the Pinebrook Club at Nichols, Connecticut, which enabled them to carry on daily preparations for their fall production. In the latter part of August I received a letter from Harold Clurman: "Are you going to be able to come out here soon? We would like you to read a script and to have time to think about it — so the earlier you come the better it will be for all of us." The script was *Johnny Johnson*.

Cheryl Crawford had persuaded Paul Green and Kurt Weill to collaborate on a play with music. Weill had composed *The Threepenny Opera* with Brecht in Berlin. This would be his Broadway debut. They produced a marriage of musical comedy and picaresque storytelling, combining poetry, burlesque, satire, and fantasy. The play, called a legend, was an imaginative portrait of recent history dramatizing the impact of World War I on Johnny Johnson, an idealistic American fighting for democracy.

The Group was a permanent company of young idealists, inventive and talented actors, eminently suited to undertake the challenge of just such a demanding work. Under the sensitive and resourceful direction of Lee Strasberg, the actors were creating a new venture out of dialogue, music, movement, and scene.

Through three acts and thirteen scenes, Green and Weill's script took off in diverse stylistic directions. The first act, with its sentimental scenes on the home front, required poetic realism to establish the nostalgia of preparations for war. The second act, with its scenes of fantasy on the battlefront, employed expressionism to present the distorted harmonies of war. In one scene the mouths of three cannon appeared above the soldiers sleeping in a dugout and complained to the audience that their iron could have been better used for machines or plowshares, "but you decreed that we must kill." The third act, with its scenes of comic satire in a psychiatric hospital, required distorted settings to reflect their mad unreality. Finally, Johnny became a pathetic pedlar, dispensing toys to children along a street symbolically leading nowhere.

In *The Fervent Years* Harold Clurman stressed that, in Group Theatre productions, "the so-called interpretive elements of the theatre were really creative functions, so that plays were to be seen as artistic wholes, not as scripts adorned by acting and direction. The true value of a production could not be adjudged simply on the basis of the writer's work." This conformed with my belief that the designer must think of the complete stage scene — the actor in a play on a stage before an audience. The designer must impress on every production a unity of visual intention. The varied stylistic values of script and music had to be organized into an artistic whole. The designer is a practical man, but also like Peter Ibbetson he must have the gift of dreaming true. At length I explained my scenic solutions to the Group's directors. They followed my line of thought and, expecting everyone to give the theatre of his best, they liked my sketches. Eagerly returning to my studio in the Times Tower to translate them into working drawings, I realized to my horror I had no sketches. I had stopped at Woolworth's to shop for some ash trays and glassware for *Stage Door* and had left my ground plans and sketches on a counter. They were never recovered!

Johnny Johnson was the seventh production which I had designed and opened on Broadway in one month. Delivering forty-one settings in four weeks was a rather pressuring schedule. And five more productions were in the planning stage. At the same time my book *Scenery Then and Now* was published and an exhibition of my drawings opened at Marie Sterner's Gallery. I also managed to conduct my classes two days every week at Yale.

Obviously something had to be done at once about *Johnny Johnson*. As a "designing man" I consoled myself with my belief that it is always just as easy to do seven or eight productions at the same time as it is to do one — barring, of course, loss of designs. Overnight I had to recall from my wretched memory those thirteen lost designs and reconstruct thirteen new thumbnail sketches. They surely had more spontaneity than the Woolworth originals.

As *Johnny Johnson* moved into high gear the production became fraught with unavoidable difficulties, and tensions rose within the Group, though they were confident they were blazing a new trail through the hurly-burly of Broadway when in 1936 experimentation was uncommon. This disturbing and poignant legend was an unconventional theatre piece, some of whose scenes shone out with glorious theatrical imagination. In the oversize Forty-Fourth Street Theatre the play appealed to the enthusiastic minority taste of the *cognoscenti* but failed to attract the larger Broadway public. It closed after sixty-eight performances.

Johnny Johnson, Minnie Belle's house

Johnny Johnson, Street and mansion

You Can't Take It With You

by Moss Hart and George S. Kaufman

Directed by Mr. Kaufman
Produced by Sam H. Harris
Booth Theatre, 1936

In the original script of *You Can't Take It with You* Moss Hart and George Kaufman contented themselves with this brief description of their play's single setting: "The room is what is customarily described as a living room, but in this house this term is something of an understatement. The everyman-for-himself room would be more like it. For here, meals are eaten, plays are written, snakes collected, ballet steps practiced, xylophones played and printing presses operated — if there were room enough, there would probably be ice-skating." There was no mention of essentials like doors, windows, and furniture.

George Kaufman as director was always more than ready to delegate authority in those areas in which he was unsure of himself. Despite his extraordinary instinct for the theatre he had little sense of the visual. He could not read a ground plan. He could not understand a sketch. A scale model confused him. He had full confidence in a few favorite designers and placed complete responsibility for settings on them.

With *You Can't Take It with You*, however, credit the authors' amiable chaotic Sycamore tribe for designing the living, dining, museumlike workroom of their house uptown in Washington Heights. The stage designer merely interpreted the happy scene of their topsy-turvy world of moonstruck lunacy. A photograph of the actual scene conveys the character of the setting more aptly than the designer's sketch. The interior architecture was minimal. The walls were old-fashioned damask wall paper, deep blue to project the accumulated treasures of the entire family. The property plot of *You Can't Take It with You* listed 742 props including 83 pictures and an assortment of exotic memorabilia:

Elephant tusk
Filipino fly whip
Tomtoms
Chinese robe
Stuffed crocodile
Russian samovar
Ship model
Piranesi print
Bowl with Japanese garden
Statue of Venus

Egyptian god
Bust of Washington
McKinley campaign medal
Human skull (candy jar)
Solarium for snakes (their hungry heads to rise on cue)
Kitten (to be replaced when it can jump off Penny's desk)

I have always designed or found my own properties. The antiques and pseudo-antiques for *You Can't Take It with You* I discovered in dark curio emporiums, art galleries, and second-hand shops under the old Second Avenue El; others I unearthed in familiar property houses and thrift shops on the West Side. Most of those picturesque haunts, like most favorite landmarks, have long since disappeared.

For my own reasons I have often introduced some object of my own into a setting, like the fragment of the Inca textile on the Sycamores' buffet. My favorite old hat has always played a disappearing act in the theatre. Long after *You Can't Take It with You* opened I found it hanging on the hatrack in the Sycamores' hallway just where I had left it weeks before. The play had settled down for a long run on the stage of the Booth Theatre, where, critic John Anderson happily observed, "every day was a neat combination of Christmas, the Fourth of July, the Fourth Dimension and April Fool's."

You Can't Take It With You, Home of Martin Vanderhof

Le Pauvre Matelot

Music by Darius Milhaud
Libretto by Jean Cocteau

Presented by the Curtis Institute of Music
Academy of Music, Philadelphia, 1937

Darius Milhaud composed *Le Pauvre Matelot* in 1927, when he was a leading member of the French modernist group, *Groupe des Six*. The work was first performed in the Opéra-Comique in Paris. Ten years later the Curtis Institute of Music gave its first American performance on the same program with the world premiere of Gian Carlo Menotti's first opera, *Amelia Goes to the Ball*. For the audience each work served as an admirable foil to the other. For the designer it was an opportunity to contrast Milhaud's dark "lament" with Menotti's *opéra bouffe* in pink and white and gold.

Le Pauvre Matelot was the sordid story of a wife who murdered her roving sailor husband unbeknown to both. It was a gruesome tale similar to so many operatic texts in vogue at that time, like Shostakovich's *Lady Macbeth of Mzensk* and Berg's *Wozzeck*. Cocteau's ironic libretto admirably served Milhaud's spare, powerful score. Vivid passages of declamation gave the work theatrical effectiveness.

The opera's action was best served by a simultaneous scene — a small bar, the sailor's house across the way, and the quay of the town. A threatening sky, engulfing the sailor's ship, overshadowed the bar. Beyond lay the placid sea. These scenic symbols sufficed to serve the acrid, restless outbursts of

Milhaud's tragic music. Scene and costumes were sketchily painted in values of black and white — haunted and tragic. For the lighting, intense colors heightened the emotional values of Cocteau's libretto and abetted the sombre mood of Milhaud's score.

Le Pauvre Matelot, Small French seaport

I'd Rather Be Right

by George S. Kaufman and Moss Hart

Music by Richard Rodgers
Lyrics by Lorenz Hart
Directed by Mr. Kaufman
Produced by Sam H. Harris
Alvin Theatre, 1937

On Wednesday, October 20, 1937, I received a hurry call from Moss Hart and George Kaufman in Boston. Their new musical show *I'd Rather Be Right* was trying out and receiving more advance publicity than any show within memory of man. Their Capitol Hill harlequinade took place in Central Park, on the Fourth of July. They were not entirely happy with their scenery. Could I design a new scene and have it ready for Baltimore in ten days? The Harris office would get the script with the ground plan to me in half an hour. I was already in the middle of three productions, including *Otello* for the Metropolitan Opera. But one more set was a challenge and I liked it. I could not, however, bring my ideas to Boston the next day, for Thursday was my day to lecture at Yale. Moss would be down next morning and meet me fifteen minutes before train time at my gate in Grand Central. I was left to dream up a new scene over night.

I'd Rather Be Right was an irreverent, glorified Gridiron show lampooning the Roosevelt administration and the New Deal. George M. Cohan was President Roosevelt. How to accommodate this contemporary political fantasy in Olmsted and Vaux's nineteenth-century Central Park? I began to imagine how the Renaissance painter Benozzo Gozzoli and Inigo Jones, an old hand at masques, might have translated Central Park's natural setting into scenery. Soon I was inventing my own fancy-free landscape, with a Vaux bridge amidst shrubs and trees, clipped and groomed and framed within a show portal of neo-Gothic pagodas and striped draperies. Everything would be light gray velour with painted accents of white, gold, and emerald green. White also for the sky and grays for translucent skyscrapers. That was my preliminary design, conceived to project the musical's high jinks and also to serve as a neutral foil for the brilliant color of the lighting and costumes.

The next morning at eight-thirty I explained my ideas to Moss Hart, who always had an unerring instinct for the visual theatre. He was understanding and seemed pleased, so I was pleased — and there we were, off on a new theatrical venture in Central Park. Isaac Benesch, my indispensable assistant for thirteen years, was present to take over, and the new scene was on the way to the drafting board while I was on my way to New Haven to impart the facts of life on scene design to my students.

The following week the new scene was rushed through McDonald's Construction Shop and the Triangle Scenic Studios. On Sunday it arrived in Baltimore, where it was set up on the stage of Ford's Theatre and lighted for the dress rehearsal that evening. With professional alacrity, choreographer Charles Weidman and director George Kaufman put the President of the United States, his Cabinet, the members of the Supreme Court, and the ladies of the ensemble through their paces in their new quarters in Central Park. That was a splendid occasion.

I'd Rather Be Right, Central Park, July 4th

Of Mice and Men

by John Steinbeck

Directed by George S. Kaufman
Produced by Sam H. Harris
Music Box Theatre, 1937

A few weeks before *Of Mice and Men* went into rehearsal, John Steinbeck attended a production conference in Sam Harris' cluttered office in the Music Box Theatre. His play was very close to the novel, so that he had very clear and definite ideas on casting, manner of speech, and movement. He went into considerable detail on scenery and costumes. At the end of the conference Steinbeck rose, said he was confident his play was in good hands and that his presence was no longer necessary. Whereupon he went out, bought a Chevrolet, and drove home to California. He never came East to see a performance of his play after it opened.

George Kaufman directed *Of Mice and Men* with perception and quiet authority. In rehearsal he always had a sensitive ear for actors' voices. He paced back and forth in the rear of the darkened auditorium, not looking at the actors, but making frightening faces to himself and listening. During the course of the play the sounds of birds, animals, night creatures, and farm life were heard beneath the human voices.

How best to visualize this poignant play, this human document which dramatizes the loneliness and the craving for affection of migrant workers on a farm along the Salinas River in California? Steinbeck was the poet of the migrant's world.

Literal as the settings must be, they must also look beneath the surface and contribute to the heartbeat of the drama. The bunkhouse of the itinerant workers is the temporary microcosm of their shifting world — beautiful in its crudeness, eloquent in its earthiness. The big barn is redolent with nostalgia for all those who have once played in such a barn. High above the haymow lonely splinters of sunlight, piercing the moted darkness, dislocate reality and transform the barn into a brooding, poetic scene for tragedy.

The sandy bank of the Salinas River opens and closes the play. This small corner of the world is the refuge of George and Lennie. Beneath the shelter of an ancient sycamore they rest, wash, build their fire, and daydream beside the river which, like their dreams, meanders away to the far horizon. The setting is a poetic melding of the sky, the tree, the river bank, and the thicket of tules — all in dusty tones of parched autumnal leaves. The scene, like the play, must radiate the lyric illusion of the essence of reality.

The river bank was mounted on one rolling platform and was as carefully detailed as a natural habitat in the Museum of Natural History. The water by the shore, with floating lily pads, was transparent plastic that raked upstage. Beneath the reflection one could see the sedges and grasses of the river bed. Just before the dress rehearsal the fire inspector insisted our river be fireproofed!

Of Mice and Men's opening night was memorable. After the final curtain, the entire audience rose spontaneously and stood in silent tribute through all the curtain calls. When the house lights came up, a salvo of cheers burst out all over the house. Months later George Kaufman recalled, "We simply came as close as we could to living up to the specifications of John Steinbeck."

Of Mice and Men, Salinas River

Otello

by Giuseppe Verdi

Directed by Herbert Graf
Conducted by Ettore Panizza
Presented by the Metropolitan Opera Association
Metropolitan Opera House, 1937

Edward Johnson planned to revive *Otello* at the Metropolitan in the late thirties after twenty-four years' absence from the repertory. He assembled a notable cast including Martinelli as Otello, Tibbett as Iago, and Rethberg as Desdemona. Adventurous Herbert Graf, whom Johnson had added to the opera's resident staff, would direct. Graf and I had done *Tristan* and *Rosenkavalier* together three seasons before in "that great experiment in opera" with the Philadelphia Orchestra.

Most of the tired productions which Mr. Johnson inherited from Gatti-Casazza's *ancien régime* had not conspicuously advanced the modern movement in the American theatre. The Metropolitan was in a financial bind. Mr. Johnson had to make do with a minimal budget in order to keep the house open. New productions were rare. During the hot summer months the stage and auditorium of the opera house were converted into a scene shop to refurbish most of those old productions. With seven operas in weekly repertory, rehearsal time onstage was insufficient. Time for lighting was minimal.

The passive attitude of the opera audience in the thirties toward the standard fare dispensed on Thirty-ninth Street was disquieting. Herbert Graf, the director, brought up in the tradition of the continental audience, expressed concern for the American opera audience. "They were curiously indiscriminating about what they saw," he recalled, "and as long as the singing was excellent, which it was most of the time, they didn't seem to mind the inadequacy of the visual side of opera. They didn't expect opera to be theatre at all, it was just opera." I too was always distressed by the way most operas looked at the Metropolitan; yet I loved the way they sounded. A few blocks north along Broadway the professional theatre's audience would not tolerate the shoddy, inept productions which nightly appeared on the Opera House stage. With our "all new" production of *Otello*, Edward Johnson, Graf, and I were determined to do something about it.

From the sweeping rise of the curtain, prefaced by no overture, our conception of presenting *Otello* was based on conventions of the theatre rather than of opera. Seldom in the musical theatre has there been such a welding of dramatic action, speech, and the sublimation of those elements in inspired song. The score of this masterpiece was Verdi at seventy-three, nevertheless writing with an intensity and passion matched by the new simplicity of his mature lyric style.

The previous spring, Herbert Graf outlined to me his scenic requirements for *Otello* — the chief entrances and exits, the ensemble relation of the principals to the massive chorus, his use of elevations for the chorus, and his basic interpretation of the musical development of the dramatic episodes. He saw the characters as human beings, active with impulsive movement, not natural gesture, believing that the greatest performers share the common ability to sing meaningfully even if they are not wholly convincing as actors in the conventional sense. Those scratchy, telegraphic lines that Graf sketched out on a pad during our working conferences recorded his directorial ideas which I would incorporate in my preliminary designs for the settings.

I visualized all four settings as highly theatrical designs that would both take on the contours of the drama and intensify its many moods. I employed color that would visualize for me the sound of music and convey to the audience specific impressions and emotions, as El Greco, Van Gogh, and Rouault did again and again using color deliberately to achieve a theatrical effect, emotion, and also to express the terrible passions of humanity.

This arbitrary use of color is not to be confused with color psychology, whose principles I have never believed were applicable to stage design, because color has such an infinite variety of connotations for us all. Take the color red. We "see" red, it is the color of blood, it implies passion, and it is also the signal for danger. Red is the color of the innermost circle of the seraphim, of Mephistopheles' cloak and the cardinal's robes, of the Communist flag and the cross of the Crusaders. In stage design the impact of red is dependent on how appropriately and imaginatively we employ it to enhance a given dramatic situation. The language of color is clearly understood on the stage when combined with the elements of form and sound.

The first act establishes the mood of the opera. The scene is Otello's castle and the harbor, caught in a raging storm whose broken shafts of light suggest the tortured emotions which eventually will shatter the protagonist. The welcoming crowds stress the dangers of the sea, whence Otello, a Moorish general in the Venetian army, arrives fresh from his latest victories and bursts into "Esultate." The storm abates. Moonlight floods the scene; and the powerful act closes serenely with the love duet of Otello and Desdemona — without color, black and white, villainy and innocence. The audience is caught up in their inevitable tragedy.

Otello's sunny workroom, in strawberry red and old white, reflects his lofty love for Desdemona.

The diagonal arched wall of the Hall of State (in a bold pattern of diapered scarlet brick) falls away in measured perspective suggesting the tragic turn of the opera. When the Venetian ambassadors announce the recall of Otello, slender columns and gold-and-ultramarine mosaic glow behind Otello's throne.

The confining walls of Desdemona's bedchamber are frescoed in smothering folds of deepest blue. Ocular windows gaze fatefully down on her canopied bed.

These backgrounds for Otello were designed some years ago. They spoke agressively for their time and circumstances.

While Otello as a lyric work of art is changeless, revivals of the opera inevitably change to reflect the changing tides of taste. In today's opera house I should certainly design Otello quite differently — with a mobile light accompaniment, more simply, more abstractly, and more symbolically, employing the analytical eye of the X-ray rather than the impressionistic lens of the camera in order to implicate the audience in even greater depth in the tragic conflict of Iago, Desdemona, and Otello.

The Fabulous Invalid

by Moss Hart and George S. Kaufman

Directed by Mr. Kaufman
Produced by Sam H. Harris
Broadhurst Theatre, 1938

Beneath his critic's robes, John Mason Brown loved the theatre's sentimental dedication to itself. He began his review of *The Fabulous Invalid* by recognizing that: "To those who are in love with it, the theatre has always been more than an art or an amusement. It has been a disease — a kind of blessed lovesickness for which there is no cure. It is a malady which eats its way into their bloodstream; an obsession which haunts their sleeping and waking hours; an illness which so affects their vision that the very word THEATRE invariably spells itself for them in capitals." Moss Hart and George S. Kaufman were long afflicted with this "blessed lovesickness" for the stage. For many years they were among her favorite suitors.

The idea for *The Fabulous Invalid* was not born suddenly. Moss Hart broached his initial notion for a play about the theatre to G. S. K. during a lull in a rehearsal of *I'd Rather Be Right*.

The Fabulous Invalid was unadorned propaganda for the living theatre, the stage, and the theatrical profession. It grew out of the authors' impulse to save the theatre, to prove that it was indestructible. Their play was a sentimental chronicle of the New York theatre, an irresistible, nostalgic cavalcade of show business since the turn of the century. Three live ghosts gave cohesion and continuity to the play's narrative. The ghosts of the two leading actors (husband and wife) and of their stage manager, all of whom dramatically died on the opening night of the Alexandria Theatre, preferred to wander through the theatre on earth because there was no theatre in heaven.

The Fabulous Invalid must be the only play in which an actual theatre is a character. The Alexandria was the star. The action covered forty years and took place all over the theatre — from the sidewalk through the lobby, into the auditorium and boxes, the orchestra pit and before the curtain, upstairs in the manager's office, backstage, in the dressing rooms, and all around the stage door.

The first scene of the play was the proud façade of New York's new Alexandria Theatre welcoming a distinguished audience on its opening night in 1900. Until 1929 this theatre traditionally offered the city "the finest in entertainment." Thereafter the Alexandria went into a decline, having survived the war, panic, the great depression, unionization, ticket speculators, even the critics. Subsequently, it succumbed in the public taste to a double-feature picture house with Screeno, and in final humiliation became a tawdry burlesque house. Ultimately, the old Alexandria closed its doors and the entrance was boarded up. In the last scene the Theatre was rescued from the wreckers by a handful of stagestruck youngsters (the Mercury or the Group Theatre?) who moved in and restored the tarnished old Alexandria with the vision of a new generation: "This isn't much of a theatre any more, but it's got a stage, and it's got seats. It's all we need."

Thirty-one changes of scene were orchestrated with nostalgic sound and music by Harry Levant. For good measure, four interludes contained a parade of sixty-five flashbacks of old songs from musicals and scenes from plays recalling memorable successes of well-loved theatre folk, from Ethel Barrymore in *Captain Jinks* (1901) to Helen Morgan in *Showboat* (1927). These passed in review, with split-second timing, within a theatre façade incorporating two stages, a projection screen, and musical accompaniment.

Obviously the play was a designer's holiday, pure pleasure twenty-four hours a day. I recall that several steel beams had to be added to the grid of the Broadhurst stage to carry the added weight of the four façades of the Alexandria. Backstage, gazing upward, Lee Shubert wryly inquired, "Are you sure they are strong enough? Don't forget, there is nothing worse than a dead actor." Did he realize the play's three principal characters were ghosts?

It is always my practice to supervise the execution of my scenery and to select and find every detail of the setting. I carry a small looseleaf notebook containing eighth-inch graph-paper ground plans and elevations with all the requirements of the scenes I am working on. With *The Fabulous Invalid* I carried a lot of scenery in my pocket!

For three weeks a photographer of *Life* Magazine trailed me all over town recording the life story of the settings for *The Fabulous Invalid*. Our daily routine included frequent visits to inspect the progress of work in construction and property shops and to approve the scene painting in the scenic studios. One old-time studio in the Bronx unearthed several ancient "used" burlesque drops. Another day we found an authentic Screeno game. Trips were scheduled to select artificial flowers, floor coverings, and fabrics, and later to check the execution of upholstery and draperies and the installation of a splendid new 1900 proscenium valance and house curtain in the Broadhurst. There were innumerable visits to the flea market on Second Avenue, property warehouses, opportunity shops, and the Salvation Army in search of gas and electric fixtures, furniture, and period decor for the manager's office and stars' dressing rooms. Other forays for props led us from Woolworth's to Macy's, even to a friendly theatre buff to wangle from him a bust of Booth and some theatrical souvenirs.

On the scheduled "load in" day, as if by magic from all over the city the theatrical impedimenta we had been accumulating were deposited on the stage of the Broadhurst Theatre. Only the designer with his pocket notebook could recognize the order in all that disorder. In two days the entire production was assembled and lights were hung and focused, ready for the light rehearsal and technical run-through on the third day. After that, the stage housing the entire Alexandria Theatre was turned over to Mr. Kaufman for dress rehearsals.

My memory of the production of *The Fabulous Invalid* was a shared experience of care and affectionate dedication. It was the professional theatre functioning at its best that made that complicated production move like clockwork.

The Fabulous Invalid was a poignant and tender salute from two of the theatre's eminent practitioners, Moss Hart and George S. Kaufman, to their successors, in imagination. It was the theatre's theatre — clever, sentimental, glamorous, and glowing with make-believe.

The Fabulous Invalid, Alexandria Theatre, Gala opening

The Fabulous Invalid, Alexandria Theatre, double feature

The Fabulous Invalid, Alexandria Theatre, closed

The American Way

by George S. Kaufman and Moss Hart

Directed by Mr. Kaufman
with Fredric March and Florence Eldridge
Produced by Sam H. Harris and Max Gordon
Center Theatre, 1939

In the late summer of 1938 all hands were deep in the production of *The Fabulous Invalid*. In the middle of a scenic conference with the authors, Moss Hart abruptly turned to George Kaufman, his voice lowered with intensity: "Shall we tell Donald about it now?" Of course I thought they were adding a new scene to the play. Quite the contrary — in breathless haste they began telling me all about *another* play they were writing, a chronicle of the nation through three generations of a German immigrant family — a patriotic cavalcade of American life with several hundred actors and innumerable realistic scenes. The first-act script would be ready the first week of October. They handed me a tentative sequence of twenty-four scenes jotted down on Moss's Hopatcong Farm stationery. "This will change, of course, but we thought you might like to be thinking about it. We'll open the middle of January." Then just as swiftly we shifted back to tackle the immediate problems of *The Fabulous Invalid*.

In October George and Moss read the first act of *The American Way* to their co-producers Sam Harris and Max Gordon. In 1938 their stirring story was a challenge to the threat of Nazism and a reaffirmation of their devotion to the fundamental ideals of freedom as a way of life in America.

Martin Gunther, a German cabinetmaker, came to America in 1895 and set up his shop in Mapleton, a typical small town in Ohio. A year later he greeted his wife and two children at Ellis Island and introduced them to the American way of life. The rest of the play took place in Mapleton. By 1914 his shop had grown into a furniture factory and he had become a prominent citizen. In 1917 his son went off to war with the AEF to fight his Fatherland. "We cannot divide our allegiance. We're no longer Germans, we are Americans," Martin told his wife. Their son was killed in action. During the Depression, trying to save a friend's bank, Martin Gunther lost his wealth but never his faith in America. Later he would die for his country by defying a secret Bund meeting and rescuing his grandson from joining the Nazis. In the final scene, all of Mapleton turned out for the funeral of their prominent fellow-citizen who so loved his country that he gave his life to preserve its ideals of democracy.

Both producers were enthusiastic about the script and agreed that this was a play whose spectacle and patriotic appeal would fill the three-thousand-eight-hundred-seat Center Theatre. That white elephant was one of the more gigantic of Broadway's cavities, built with Radio City Music Hall in Rockefeller Center as popular cultural showcases for ballet, opera, musicals, and pictures. Now for the first time Kaufman and Hart were writing a play with a specific theatre in mind.

The producers mapped out their production plans on a large scale. George Kaufman of course would stage the production, but, because of his shyness working with large numbers of actors, George Heller would direct the crowds. Fredric March and Florence Eldridge were engaged for the principal roles. Hassard Short was signed to coordinate the lighting and technical direction. Oscar Levant would arrange the music and also conduct it from a studio seven stories above the stage. Irene Sharaff would design some twenty-two hundred costumes. I was to design the scenery and to convert the huge Center Theatre into a theatre for drama.

The orchestra pit was raised to create a stepped forestage in order to bring the action of the play closer to the audience. A new proscenium was installed to frame the new forestage and also to conform with the existing circular wooden auditorium. New lighting and an effective sound projection system brought the auditorium into scale and harmony with the play.

With no side-stage storage space, the front-stage elevator would convey bulky scenery and props to the basement for storage. In designing the seventeen scenes of the play, careful consideration was given to the technical solutions of shifting and storing the sets, which included many interiors and exteriors — Ellis Island, the Country Club, the Bund meeting in a grove, the Fourth of July picnic grounds, and Mapleton's main square.

Many of the spectacular episodes of *The American Way* took place in the elm-shaded main square of Mapleton embracing its Civil War monument. Here were the 1896 campaign parades and political rallies for Bryan and McKinley, and later the townfolks' welcome-home parade for the victorious heroes returning from France in 1919. Here in the dark days of the Depression a mob of citizens caused a run on the Mapleton National Bank. Here in 1939 the town turned out to pay homage to their martyred first citizen.

My design for Mapleton's main square was derived from a collection of hundreds of old picture postcards of small American towns I discovered in the New York Public Library. That source material revealed that main squares the country over between 1895 and 1939 had suffered little change, from dusty street to asphalt, from hitching post to parking meter — except for the inevitable transformation of stores and business houses. The sign "Harness & Buggy Shop" became "Automobile Parts." A soda fountain was downgraded to a bar and later to a filling station. The shoeshine parlor under the Mapleton Hotel became a cocktail lounge, and next door the cigar store's Indian surrendered to a neon sign. A bakery became a chain store, and Mercer's Bazaar was transformed into the Bijou Movie Theatre. My real problem was to create the illusion of Mapleton's spacious main square within the limited space of the Center Theatre's stage, so that the square could not only accommodate the cast of two hundred fifty but also make those actors appear to be thousands of Mapletonians.

The finale of *The American Way* was pure theatre — tense and patriotic. When Martin Gunther's funeral procession moved from the church through the main square, "The Star-Spangled Banner" was heard faintly sung by a few citizens, but it soon grew into a great crescendo that brought the vast audience to its feet too choked to move. "Few there could have failed to see in that frankly tear-stained moment," recorded John Anderson on the opening night, "that the audience had become a part of the play, and the play a part of us, or failed to realize that this final gesture the audience made was larger than the playhouse, as large, indeed, as a continent and an ideal."

The American Way, Mapleton outing

89

The American Way, Statue of Liberty

The American Way, Parade

Prometheus Bound

by Aeschylus

Translated by Edith Hamilton
Directed by Constance Welsh
Yale School of Drama, 1939

We are in the theatre watching a rehearsal of *Prometheus Bound* on a bare stage. Center stage, sitting in an old armchair, is the actor who is to play Prometheus, who first gave light and fire to man. "Behold what I, a god, endure from gods." We soon forget that he is a man dressed as we are, moving as we do. He has become a kind of Presence, always there dominating the stage. He grows in stature before our very eyes. And there, always encircling him, is the Chorus. We ourselves, like the Chorus, are attendant witnesses.

What classical scenery on our stage today can best serve the suspended action of this play which in rehearsal seemed so well served by a bare stage? A scene of haunting solitude is needed, for Prometheus has been denied even the companionship of moving clouds and rain and stars. This scene must transform the actor into a medium for the expression of tense emotional power, just as Artur Rubinstein fills a great bare stage with the authority of his music.

William Blake once sketched a spacious empty room and set within it a small sanctuary with a figure beneath a lamp, lighted. He called it "Vision." For our scene, then, let there be a lofty room, timeless, ageless, whose transparent walls, without door or window, are gray gauze. Also the costumes are gray like the clay Plato tells us Prometheus fashioned us of. This harmoniously ordered chamber, confining Prometheus within the citadel of his conscience, will dramatize his lonely resignation more vividly than the most remote summit of the Caucasus. Beyond the confining walls is the unfettered region of outer space, symbolizing Prometheus' unbroken spirit.

Mobile light animates the action of the drama, flooding the chamber with life or leaving it an awesome vacuum. In the opening scene Hephaestus, Force, and Power bind Prometheus to his rock, "where no man ever comes, where never voice or face of mortal you will see." The source of light is contained within the chamber while the attendant Chorus of Oceanides first respond to Prometheus' tragic fate. During the subsequent confrontations of Oceanus, Io, and Hermes with Prometheus, conflicting lights invade the chamber from within and from without. As Prometheus' will to endure his fate strengthens, the supporting light from without increases and pervades the scene. At length Prometheus defies Zeus' authority and with resignation he cries out, "On me the tempest falls." The all-consuming blinding light of godhead crashes about him and the scene is engulfed in darkness. "It does not make me tremble," asserts Prometheus, and from his bound body glows a radiant light symbolizing the triumph of the forces of right. "O holy Mother, O air and sun, behold me, I am wronged." In answer an all-embracing curtain in folds of warm light descends like a healing epilogue over the sanctuary of Prometheus and concludes the drama.

Prometheus Bound, William Blake's "Vision"

Prometheus Bound

94

Prometheus Bound

The Old Foolishness

by Paul Vincent Carroll

Presented by John Golden
Directed by Rachel Crothers
Windsor Theatre, 1940

Paul Vincent Carroll was a mystic writer who confessed, "The only way I know of portraying certain human forces on the stage is through symbols." He succeeded brilliantly in his two earlier plays, *Shadow and Substance* and *The White Steed*.

The Old Foolishness is an allegorical play about the intangibles that lie above reality. The play is a version of the Pelleas and Melisande story wrapped up in the graceful and picturesque trappings of the Gaelic theatre. Melisande is the bewitched and bewitching Celtic siren who symbolizes the spirit of Ireland. Maeve's lovers are three brothers, farm folk of County Down. To Carroll they portray the three most important manifestations of Irish life, the soldier, the scholar, and the man of the land.

In the second act Maeve invades the eerie ruins of an ancient castle atop the Mourne Mountains. It is a mystical meeting place for lovers — "suspended between peaks of ecstasy" — open to the moon and stars and boldly romantic, yet austere and tragical. One critic felt, "Mr. Carroll's noble premises made pedestrian people and their words seem mere poetic trespassers." Perhaps that is why they seemed intruders in this poetic setting where Maeve discovered neither happiness nor understanding with her lovers and the following day, for her own exalted reasons, took her lonely leave from their farmhouse at the foot of the mountains.

With all the care that was lavished on the preparation of the production, *The Old Foolishness* departed from the Windsor Theatre after three performances.

The Old Foolishness, Ruins of Irish castle

The Doctor's Dilemma

by George Bernard Shaw

Presented by Katharine Cornell
Directed by Guthrie McClintic
With Miss Cornell and Raymond Massey
Shubert Theatre, 1941

Katharine Cornell told how "Guthrie came home one night rather late with a book and when I asked him what it was he told me it was something he would like to read me after dinner." Later that evening, after reading *The Doctor's Dilemma,* "We decided suddenly that it was the thing to do and although we only spent a few weeks getting it in shape, sudden decisions frequently result in greater success than those which are carefully deliberated and take several months to plan."

Shaw wrote *The Doctor's Dilemma* in answer to a challenge from William Archer that he couldn't turn out a play about death. He retorted that he would make it a comedy, not a tragedy. And he did so, slapping down the whole medical profession in the process. Shaw's lampoon was rich in men's roles, and Katharine Cornell surrounded herself with an impressive cast of almost all the notable British talent in this country. Her concern was for the play, rather than the significance of her own role of Jennifer Dubedat.

Guthrie McClintic, with his innate enthusiasm for the theatre, always brought taste to their productions. In our discussions of the scenes we hoped to revive the dignity and style of the Edwardian theatre without dwarfing its stature. We wanted to create new memories instead of challenging old ones.

Preparing a production with Kit and Guthrie was always an adventure. While their managers, Gertrude Macy and Stanley Gilkey, had an ever-sharp eye to economy, everything had to be the best. Almost always there was much shifting of furniture back and forth between Broadway and the McClintics' Beekman Place house. It might be a desk, a table, a stool. There were two favorite Regency armchairs that served sentimentally in almost every one of their productions after *The Barretts of Wimpole Street.* These were good "acting" chairs. Miss Cornell referred to their town house as "a sort of domestic museum of our careers in the theatre." It had pieces of furniture from most of their plays. "At odd moments when we thought we could afford something really nice for the house we would buy it. Then would come that awful moment when we knew it would be perfect for a stage set and off it would go working — like a theatrical child." While they loved their houses in Beekman Place and Sneden's Landing on the Hudson and on a beach at Martha's Vineyard, their real home was the theatre.

For the three realistic interiors of *The Doctor's Dilemma,* I proposed we adopt the turn-of-the-century tradition of painted scenery — and with fresh color, beautiful furnishings, atmospheric lighting, and Motley's chic clothes, make that tradition stylish and theatrical today. This design approach was appropriate to the period of the play, economical to build and paint, and easy to shift. The scenic artist's brush became mightier than the builder's hammer. Painted light and shade, whether in architectural detail or natural foliage, achieved a more three-dimensional illusion of reality than the real thing.

For the terrace of the Star and Garter Inn, Shaw describes in detail the position of the chairs and the actors around the dinner table. For the rest, his description is atmospheric: "A cloudless summer night; nothing disturbs the stillness except from time to time the long trajectory of a distant train and the measured clucking of oars coming up from the Thames in the valley below." An ancient half-timber inn framed a panoramic translucent drop showing the moonlit Thames meandering through horizontal patterns of meadows and low-lying hills toward the distant sky. Dubedat gazing out over this view remarked, "I've just been making a little note of the river tonight; it will work into something good. . . . I think I'll call it the Silver Danube." The silver of the Thames in the foreground merged with the tablecloth. In this way the white chairs and the table with the doctors in evening dress, a white bench around a painted tree, and pale flowers on a painted balcony were subtly interrelated to establish a calculated theatrical effect.

For the picture gallery in Bond Street our scene was a spacious nineteenth-century salon whose elegance would serve as an appropriate foil for the final confrontation between Jennifer and Dr. Ridgeon. A high, curtained arch of bird's-eye maple separated the scene's more intimate foreground, in red and gold, from the picture gallery in the rear, whose beige walls were hung with framed pictures, "painted" in perspec-tive, of the fashionable artists Conder, Crane, and Sickert. A central partition appropriately displayed a show of Dubedat's work. An easel held a picture that had been prominent in his studio.

The intention was to express in scenic terms Jennifer's idealized image of her deceased artist-husband with his work so in evidence that the gallery appeared to be dedicated to his memory in the same spirit as the book she had written about him.

I think all of us working on this production of Shaw's comedy about death were challenged with his glowing message delivered by Dubedat, an unscrupulous artist with high gifts, who, as he lay dying in his studio, proclaimed: "I believe in . . . the might of design, the mystery of color, the Redemption of all things by Beauty everlasting, and the message of Art that has made these hands blessed."

The Doctor's Dilemma, Terrace of the Star and Garter

The Doctor's Dilemma, Art gallery, Bond Street

Job

A Theatrical Presentation of the Book of Job
Based on the Adaptation of Norman Corwin

A Project, 1941

The designer is not always happy or satisfied with doing merely what he is asked to do in the Broadway theatre. Sometimes he must also do what something within himself insists that he get done. I had always wanted to do a modern production of the Old Testament drama of Job — high theatre and noble verse. That was why, even though I was busy designing ten productions during the Broadway season of 1940–1941, I sat down and made my own dramatic arrangement of the Book of Job and then, for my own edification and diversion, devised a series of designs for the production.

In this project for *Job,* I sought to extend the idiom of the theatre. As with Artaud, it was not my intention to conceal the devices of the theatre, but to make them deliberately obvious. My setting indicates neither time nor place. However, through the course of the play run recurring allusions to lightness and darkness and significant references to circles and spheres.

In the beginning, two Readers are sitting downstage right and left on a sweeping arc, like two sibyls, reading to us from their massive books about Job and his family:

There was a man whose name was Job and that man was perfect and upright, God-fearing and without evil.

Within the central luminous sphere a heroic shadow of Job himself appears. The Readers continue:

Now on the day when the Sons of God came to gather round the Lord, Satan also came with them.

Quivering radial lights of the Sons of God encircle the glowing light of God, against which the symbolic shadow of Satan suggests a minor eclipse. The play begins with the dialogue between the Lord and Satan over testing Job's steadfast faith through his trial and tribulation.

My basic design for *Job* is founded on symbology — of the sphere representing the individual, of space representing man's solitary course in light and time. On occasion the sphere appears to liberate the spirit, or space appears confined by the forces confronting Job. Irised within a circular frame, the entire drama is confined to the sloping disk of a revolving, truncated cone which completes one revolution during the course of the play. The disk provides unity of action. It is a sculptor's rotating pedestal on which Job and his three companions, like living statues modeled in clay, are spotlighted against changing light images. These images are Job's tortured visions "externalized" — the anguished inner conflict of his self-justification.

In 1941 I conceived of *Job* as a dynamic production integrating poetry, mime, sound, and light. The mobile light forms that accompany the drama were to be projected on the surrounding cyclorama. I was well aware that light projections could never rebound from the surface of the cyclorama into space, although ideally I had thought of these images as three-dimensional light forms. I envisioned the Voice of the Lord and the Voice of Satan as spheres of light addressing one another and sharing the cubic space of the stage with the actors.

I have always felt the designer must know more about light — not in terms of electronics or the physics of light, but closer rapport should exist between the lighting engineer in his laboratory and the theatre artist in his studio. They both share common interests. They both explore and experiment. Over the years we have requested from lighting engineers new and improved equipment to simplify our work in the theatre. Within reason, they have provided it. Today it remains for the playwright, the director, and the designer to discover more about light as drama, about light as a tangible substance, about tempering and converting the potential of this force to more imaginative dramatic uses in theatre and television.

In 1941 I dreamed of light only as a body occupying stage space like actors and plastic scenery. Now I can see the theatre is on the threshold of an optical breakthrough perhaps as significant as was the formula of perspective in the theatre of the Renaissance. The concept of light as scenery existing in space is within our grasp through the medium of holography. The technique of holography was first conceived by the British scientist Dennis Gabor in 1948. Since the development of the laser beam a few years later, holography has made great strides. Peggy Sealfon in her illuminating article in *The New York Times* for May 11, 1975, pointed out that holography, practically a stepchild of photography, is a phenomenon that can be explained by understanding the nature of light. The three-dimensional hologram or light image can be projected in space by means of lenses, mirrors, and film, with two laser beams (or mercury arcs) as a source of light. Where the two beams meet, a light interference pattern is formed and this is recorded. The hologram is still in its experimental stages of development. The universities would seem to be the appropriate institutions to effect a collaboration between the scientific laboratories and the visual and performing arts. They are in a position to conduct creative investigation in the infinite capabilities of the hologram and to adapt their three-dimensional findings to imaginative use in the visual arts, the theatre, and television.

Today my project for *Job* could be far more dramatically realized by employing the medium of holography. The majestic voice and the eye of God could burst forth from the whirlwind in an actual blaze of light and confront Job standing in darkness:

Who then is he that can stand before me?
Whatsoever is under the whole heaven is mine!

And Job, prostrating himself in final humility before the luminous presence of the Lord God, repents:

I uttered things I did not understand,
Things far beyond me, of which I had no knowledge.
From hearsay only had I heard of Thee,
But verily now mine eyes have seen Thee.
Therefore, I recant and in dust and ashes do repent.

The whirlwind subsides. The light of the Almighty vanishes, and myriads of stars in circular order appear in the depth of a lustrous sky. And the balance between circles and spheres and man's course in lightness and darkness and time is restored. The two Readers who in the beginning introduced Job now conclude the drama:

And the Lord turned the wheel of Job's fortune. And all of his relations and his former friends heard these good things that had befallen Job and came to feast with him in his house.

Job

Job

Job

Job

Job

As You Like It

by William Shakespeare

An Unrealized Production by the Theatre Guild
For Katharine Hepburn, 1941

In 1941, Theresa Helburn and Lawrence Langner planned a Shakespeare Festival for the Theatre Guild. They commissioned me to design the scenes and costumes for *As You Like It* with Katharine Hepburn playing Rosalind. Their plans for the festival failed to materialize. Only a brief correspondence and a few sketches survive to record this project.

Today, in our theatre, how does the designer address himself to "the great classic voice of the English-speaking theatre"? Originally Shakespeare was produced without benefit of scenery; his stage was a permanent architectural arrangement that projected into an open auditorium lighted by the sun. On that bare stage Shakespeare established the illusion of locale with the poetry he assigned to his players. Since then fourteen generations of actors, designers, and directors have used Shakespeare's plays as a challenge to test their talents. Many of the theatre's most memorable productions have been those created for his plays, and they in turn have contributed to the course of the theatre advancing.

The first folios of Shakespeare do not describe the plays' scenes. They are merely indicated — Act I, Scene 1; Act II, Scene 2. So the scene designer begins his work by making soundings in the hearts of the characters of the play, by observing their actions in dramatic conflict. What kind of costumes will Rosalind and Celia wear when they retreat from the court to the Forest of Arden, masquerading as the rustics Ganymede and Aliena? With the director, the designer determines the essential lines of the plot that are to be emphasized — naturalistic, melodramatic, psychologic, symbolic. What outward atmosphere best serves the needs of the inner drama? The designer's instinct for the play will enable him to determine the direction away from realism the production will take. His compass of intuition will guide him toward a style of production, so that when the curtain rises, the audience will realize that this production of *As You Like It* is no ordinary eyewitness affair. The Forest of Arden indeed is the "golden world" of the Duke's exiled court and of eight disparate lovers. The play's many settings have been wrought from the hearts of the characters who will inhabit them. While the designer has made these scenes one with the actors, he has also identified them with the audience's imagination.

What kind of trees flourished in the Forest of Arden — oak, palm, greenwood? Is it like Windsor Forest or the Forest of Fontainebleau, a grove of sequoias, or a version of the Garden of Eden? How differently every artist has always envisioned his trees — the miniature trees of a medieval illuminator; the poetic, Gothic trees of William Blake; the prismatic constructions of Cézanne. The stage designer's arboretum contains all these trees from the past and many more of his own theatrical invention, like the mighty ash tree of Hunding's hut in the *Walküre*, the guardian twin elms that brood over the Cabot farmhouse in *Desire Under the Elms*, or the magical trees that wither in Klingsor's enchanted garden in *Parsifal*.

Think of *As You Like It* as a masque in which the Duke and his followers have been banished from his own court (by his usurper brother) to an umbrageous retreat in the Forest of Arden. The Duke vividly conjures up this forest of enchantment — indeed he begins to design it!

And this our life, exempt from public haunt,
Finds tongues in trees, books in the running brooks,
Sermons in stones, and good in everything:
I would not change it.

Rustic pavilions right and left against richly foliated drapes and leafy swags frame the forest, whose trees are poetic symbols of trees summoned to the stage by Shakespeare's characters. Orlando hangs upon a tree a verse in witness of his love for Rosalind, and gazing up into the leafy canopy cries out:

O Rosalind! these trees shall be my books,
And in their barks my thoughts I'll character;
That every eye, which in this forest looks,
Shall see thy virtue witness'd everywhere.

These "versified" trees addressed to Rosalind must strike a chord of recognition in "every eye" in the audience. For the rustic banquet scene, shadows of trees are bedecked with garlands of laurel leaves. In another part of the forest, Rosalind and Orlando are lovers lost amidst pale concealing trees, with the lovers' moon lost, too, high among the tree tops. In an early palace scene the usurper's courtiers, attired in red and russet, attend the fateful wrestling match between Orlando and Charles in a foliated cockpit of white and gold.

As You Like It is a masquerade in which the banished Duke and his masquers, living "like the old Robin Hood," discover rustic revelry, and a "life more sweet than that of painted pomp" in their enchanted Forest of Arden.

As You Like It, Forest

Pygmalion

by George Bernard Shaw

Presented by Theatre Incorporated
Staged by Cedric Hardwicke
With Gertrude Lawrence and Raymond Massey
Ethel Barrymore Theatre, 1945

During my isolation from Broadway on Guam, I had decided to give up the theatre. In 1945 I spent my terminal leave from the AAF arranging my new industrial design office. My first inquiring phone call was not from a tycoon seeking a new look for his products, but from an old associate of many productions, Richard Aldrich, who was managing director of a new group called Theatre, Inc. They were planning as their first Broadway production a revival of Shaw's *Pygmalion,* directed by Cedric Hardwicke with Gertrude Lawrence and Raymond Massey. "We all want you to design the scenes, Don." "But," I retorted, "I'm out of the theatre. I'm an industrial designer now!" In his paternal way Dick reassured me: "That can wait. You can design for industry right after *Pygmalion* opens. I'll send a script right over." The next day I was back in the theatre again — reinflated after three and a half years of war and a brief skirmish with industrial design. I was working with an adventurous young theatre group who would have no compromise with quality. Norris Houghton, one of the founders of Theatre, Inc., stated their case: "The founders are convinced that there are persons who believe, as they do, that the theatre is an end in itself, that, freed from the fettering impositions which money-making forces onto creative enterprise, it can take its place alongside opera and ballet and symphony orchestras as a proper object of philanthropic support." The founders had already raised their nonprofit revolving fund and were going into rehearsal in several weeks.

Shaw took the title for his comedy from the Latin poet Ovid, who recounted how the sculptor Pygmalion created a beautiful statue and then fell in love with it. Shaw does not quite have Henry Higgins fall in love with Eliza, the Cockney flower girl, whom he discovers late one evening under the portico of St. Paul's Church; but Higgins does declare, "I can make a duchess of her in six months." And that is the story of the play.

My design for the prologue was a rather free variant of Shaw's description of the set, which placed Inigo Jones's façade of St. Paul's Church upstage, and thus forced the actors to play their scenes downstage amidst the frantic confusion of Covent Garden traffic and torrents of rain. Cedric Hardwicke, an accomplished old hand with Shaw's plays, agreed with my proposal to place the portico downstage raised on a two-foot platform the full width of the stage. This plan kept the actors under the shelter of the portico and out of the traffic, and required a minimum of "real" rain. Center steps between Inigo Jones's "painted" Etruscan columns led down to the street. Beyond there stretched away in perspective a translucent backdrop of Covent Garden Market skylights with lamps and the stalls reflected in the wet streets. That shallow scene gave the illusion of three-dimensional reality, yet it was economically achieved. At the close of the scene, Gertrude Lawrence hailed a profile taxicab upstage, entered, and drove off toward the first experiment in her new life. The portico platform and all of Covent Garden were flown, thus making the scene change to Higgins' consulting room in twenty seconds — long before the arrival of Eliza in her taxicab.

Pygmalion, Portico

Born Yesterday

by Garson Kanin

Presented by Max Gordon
Staged by Mr. Kanin
With Judy Holliday and Paul Douglas
Lyceum Theatre, 1946

Born *Yesterday* was one of the hilarious social comedies of the forties. Garson Kanin wrote and directed it. "When one has lived and worked as long as I have," Garson has maintained, "one comes to the realization that the best part of one's life is the working part, the creative part." A close working partnership on a production with Garson Kanin has always been a stimulating experience for me as a designer. He likes to exercise his talents and take off in fresh directions.

Born Yesterday required a single setting — a deluxe suite in a Washington hotel for which a junk-dealer-turned-millionaire paid $235 per day back in 1946 to house his entourage. Such an opulent, eye-filling hotel room with five entrances on several levels posed a problem. The audience must see it is expensive and believe it, but once the curtain has gone up the setting must become an unobtrusive background. The stage setting for *Born Yesterday* is like a show window in which to display the production of the play. If it projects the playwright's intentions, as a successful window display projects a piece of merchandise, then the setting makes its point.

While I always think of a setting in terms of plan, I visualize simultaneously the scene growing before me in elevation. The designer must imagine and think in terms of scale. I prefer to work in a small scale — $\frac{1}{8}'' = 1'$ — and on ordinary graph paper. The graph paper controls me and enables me to control my design. It helps me to think practically and swiftly in terms of space. With a few pencil strokes I can revise an entire design, snare new ideas, and set them down on the squared paper before me. I find this is a contained yet flexible way to explore all the design possibilities of a setting.

For *Born Yesterday* the free curvaceous line of the Baroque provided the plan with an organic unity like a conch shell or a machine with its interconnecting parts. This is evident in the staircase, its landings, and the window alcove. In the architectural extrusion of mantel, doors, and extravagant stair rail, I chose to exaggerate the flamboyant "modern Baroque" style made so fashionable during the forties in New York, Chicago, and San Francisco by the distinguished decorator Dorothy Draper. This was repeated in a glass Spanish mirror hanging above the mantel on a marbleized wall, in a photo mural of an Italian Baroque drawing for a stage scene by Juvara, in a modern Swedish cabinet, in the curves of Austrian chairs, tables, chandeliers. Finally the curve attained climactic expression in the dome of the Capitol seen through the circular bay alcove.

Color can play a meaningful theatrical role in an interior setting. The architectural detail and furnishings were in old white and dark plum, dramatic against muted greige walls. The designer's theatrical palette for a successful play like *Born Yesterday* may sometimes establish a trend in contemporary interior decor. The toned-down display of the setting's splashy grandeur complemented the disordered life style of the happy denizens who occupied the scene. The setting was conceived as subtle good-humoured parody — a scenic satire. Many in the audience responded to this hotel suite of an Al Capone of big business and thought it was very "beautiful." And that was the idea.

Born Yesterday, Hotel suite

The Abduction from the Seraglio

by Wolfgang Amadeus Mozart

Presented by the Metropolitan Opera Association
Conducted by Emil Cooper
Directed by Herbert Graf
Metropolitan Opera House, 1946

In the last quarter of the eighteenth century, the Middle East was an exotic and alien world to the artists, writers, and composers of Western Europe. *The Abduction from the Seraglio* was one of the first enduring musical works set in this fascinating world. Mozart, working on the score, recounted how he was living in such an Oriental state of imagination that the color of Turkomania permeated his score. The opera is small-scale. Its appeal lies in the charm and elegance of the music and in the exacting arias that demand virtuoso singing of the highest order.

In 1945, Frank St. Leger, Herbert Graf, and I proposed a production in English of *The Abduction from the Seraglio* to adventurous Frank Ricketson, Jr., president of the Board of the Central City Opera House Association in Colorado. The following year, with St. Leger as producer, our project was realized with Eleanor Steber singing Constanza in the mile-high opera house whose twenty-five-foot proscenium accommodated Mozart's intimate opera perfectly. We sought to depart from the rococo tradition of the opera's first performance in Vienna in 1782. We expanded the scenic sequences of the opera from three acts in two scenes to three acts in nine scenes in order to make the production breathe and move more freely.

For the Oriental decor and costumes of *The Seraglio* I invaded the ancient forbidden pleasure domes of the Middle East — Turkey, Arabia, and Persia. This eclectic approach would bring a quality of fantasy to the visual style of the production, hopefully similar to Mozart's fancy-free employment of "Turkish music." The permanent setting was a theatrical interpretation of a Persian miniature. The decorative frame, the garden, the lake above, and higher still the sky, were flat planes arranged in perpendicular projection without regard to literal perspective. These planes were acting levels on which Herbert Graf deployed his cast with fine pictorial finesse. A low central level and lacquer railings broke up the scale of the wide front stage and made the acting areas an integral part of the total stage picture. A cobalt traveler curtain, flecked with the same Persian clouds as the portal, displayed the two palaces of the captive ladies Constanza and Blonda. As in the musical theatre, this show curtain gave momentum and variety to the movement of the opera. Some of the arias were sung in front of the curtain while a new scene was being set behind it. All of the scenes fitted into specific areas of the permanent setting. They were flat and stylized, merely painted indications of Orientalia. A wall with a door for the entrance to the Pasha's palace, a canopy or a miniature pavilion for a garden, a Moorish arch for Constanza's apartment, a Turkish grill for a prison. Costumes and scenery seemed proud of their bright eclecticism and artifice, and of their integration with the "Turkish music" of Mozart's beguiling opera.

Our altitudinal production was so well received by Central City that Edward Johnson, whose Metropolitan schedule was quite flexible in those days, asked Graf and me to reproduce our production the following November. This would be the first time (after 164 years) for *The Abduction from the Seraglio* at the Metropolitan Opera. On that huge stage our challenging task was to double the scale of our original production yet preserve the intimacy so essential to Mozart's work which we had achieved in Central City.

The Abduction from the Seraglio, Oriental garden

Land's End

by Thomas Job

Presented by Paul Feigay and George Somnes
Staged by Robert Lewis
The Playhouse, 1946

Land's End is the Tristan and Isolde legend cast in a contemporary dramatic mold. It is a tragedy of brooding enchantment whose ill-fated lovers and fisherfolk inhabit the Cornish coast at the westernmost tip of England. This is an austere land of ancient folk tales and mysterious carved rune stones. The cliffs and the ruined castle of Tristan hang in the air alone "like brooding fates," dominating the many settings of the play.

These scenes must evoke the atmosphere of the play and create in the minds of the audience a living mood — their own inner sense of time and place. I wanted the scenes to establish a heightened kind of artificiality — "to capture not verisimilitude but reality," as Thornton Wilder sought to achieve it in dismissing conventional scenery in his early plays. In all the scenes of the play, the rocks, the sea, the sky, and man's habitations were all in tonalities of gray-blue and gray — but seeming of one substance. This imparted an air of generalized truth to the reality of the scenes.

The Men-on-Thol is an ancient monument overlooking the sea and the cliffs of Land's End. Dawn finds the lovers drawn like victims to this primitive site. At the climactic moment of their scene the rising sun strikes the round rune stone and, piercing the stone's eye, magically transfixes the two lovers against the uprearing megalithic rock — the essence of drama today, even as in the timeless beginnings of drama.

Land's End, Hotel Cornwall dining room

The Leading Lady

by Ruth Gordon

Presented by Victor Samrock and William Fields
Directed by Garson Kanin
With Miss Gordon
National Theatre, 1948

Ruth Gordon has always had the conviction that the theatre is the most wonderful place in the world. From her childhood years in Wollaston, Massachusetts, she yearned to go on the stage.

She wrote *The Leading Lady* and played the title role, the wife in a distinguished costarring team on Broadway at the turn of the century. Out of her great knowledge of and affection for the theatre, as playwright and player, she brought forth its magic make-believe in a play of great heart.

The scene of the play is the drawing room of Gay and Gerald Marriott's house at 60 West 27th Street, New York City, at an after-the-theatre party, on New Year's Eve, 1899. After twenty years or more of costarring, they are celebrating the successful opening of their newest play. Theatrical celebrities and artists are all there, including Clyde Fitch working on *Captain Jinks of the Horse Marines* at the piano. Mainbocher designed the play's glamorous costumes, which dramatically recalled the elegant manners of an earlier era.

The Leading Lady's single setting had to do some quiet acting on its own. First the scene had to recapture the nostalgic gaiety, brilliance, and heartbeat of the theatre at the turn of the century. At the climactic finish of the party scene, Gerald falls into a mortal swoon after a display of jealous temper with Gay. Thereafter through the remainder of the play the drawing room records the downward course of Gay's prestigious career through flops and failures. She must sell her antiques, pawn her jewels, and convert her once splendid home into a theatrical boarding house.

The Marriotts' gray-paneled drawing room, with their portraits by Sargent and Whistler, reflected the spacious air of the houses that once graced Stuyvesant Square and Gramercy Park. French furniture in petit-point and vitrines with theatrical curios graced an Aubusson carpet. Center stage a Victorian conversation piece in red damask held the room together. Garson Kanin employed this piece as a focal point to great advantage. Overhead the frescoed ceiling reflected the warmth of gas brackets and flickering candles in a crystal chandelier. A lighted Christmas tree and holly decked the room, and Tiffany silver vases were filled with American Beauty roses. Supper was served in the adjoining palm-lined solarium.

Through the play the grandeur of this room diminishes and is dismantled before the audience's eyes as Gay Marriott's fortune dwindles — a great actress of another era who had begun as a chambermaid in Chicago's Palmer House — and finally rises and triumphs in her later years.

When I arrived at the Selwyn Theatre in Chicago to assemble the scene for the tryout, I came upon a great surprise. It was a one-and-only time for the designer. It would never happen again. There on the theatre marquee in lights were "Mainbocher" and "Oenslager" along with Garson Kanin and Ruth Gordon. I like to believe they had cooked up the idea with the producers Vic Samrock and Bill Fields to mark with a little light the particular happy collaboration we shared together in the production of *The Leading Lady* — an expression of the same deep feeling for the theatre that Ruth Gordon was dreaming of back in Wollaston before she arrived on Broadway.

The Leading Lady, Drawing room, 1899

Life With Mother

by Howard Lindsay and Russel Crouse

Produced by Oscar Serlin
With Dorothy Stickney and Mr. Lindsay
Directed by Guthrie McClintic
Empire Theatre, 1948

Notes for *Life With Mother.*
These notes are reproduced line for line from Mr. Oenslager's work sheets.

LWM sequel 7½ yrs — Nov 1939 — 47
charmed 8 million people
Day family National characters,
Fresh funny as ever — saga of the house of Clarence Day
embattled domesticity
It has charm — 1880's lovable people
Vinnie & ~~Faulkne~~ Father — accent on the distaff side
Characters have become American Institutions
sentimental humors of a fascinating family life
set just far enough back in American history to be credible
sturdy artful and lucid (director) inventive
relish warmth & humor touching with nostalgic flavor
Happy return of the Days — tumultuous household
* * * * * * * * * * ? predecessor — ~~about~~
As Father would say stomping about, "Oh, Ga-a-ahd?
It's good to have them back in town again!"
"LWM is a comedy full of those minor crises,
a comedy of fresh and beguiling touches,
sagacious and unforgettable bits (twists) on writing,
and in the play and in the director"
Barbara Bulgakov Moscow Art Theatre called it "Stylized Fun"

country place
a big airy living room with plenty of places for flowers
cool country house and the warm town house
City House set for LWF is New York City
Act III 1–2) The morning room of the Day House
During the early days of the record-breaking
run (7½ yrs) of *Life With Father* Howard Lindsay and
Russel Crouse were already dreaming up new joys
and sorrows for the Day family with some caution for
sequels in the theatre are notoriously disillusioning
At long last the play was finished in 1948. All the critics
agreed they had dispelled the jinx.

1 — After LWF — writing a successor — Quote L & S
2. The Family — The Comedy
3. Stewart Chaney
3. [4.] The Setting and Costumes

Creams and gilt woodwork with pink walls and pinker
cottage woven damask panels
Mantel face panels decorated with plum blossoms
on a blue sky background
American Empress and Victorian (Wicker) furniture
Flowers everywhere.
Curtains lace with over drapes of pink and white chintz
An ivory replica of the Taj Mahal
Victorian Porch with tasseled green and white striped
    awnings.
Hall — Victorian — _____? gray and yellow.
Ottoman — Vinnie in blue

Life With Mother, Set detail

Life With Mother, First and second act set drawing

Life With Mother, Production photo

Life With Mother is the last text completed by Mr. Oenslager before his death.
The following pages illustrate works that he had intended to discuss.

The Temporary Mrs. Smith, City skyline

The Beautiful Galatea, Stage model

Dido and Aeneas, Forest

Coriolanus, Permanent set

The Ballad of Baby Doe, Clarendon Hotel

The Ballad of Baby Doe, "Vote for W. J. Bryan"

Major Barbara, Slums

Major Barbara, Perivale St. Andrews

Mary Stuart, Fotheringay Park

"J. B."

Orfeo, Plains of Thrace

A Call on Kuprin, Russian riverbank

First Love

First Love, Set model

Tosca, Cathedral scene model

A Masked Ball, Ground row, Ramps gallows

Antigone, Set

Don Carlos, The garden, Monastery of St. Just

Projects Designed by Donald Oenslager

1924   *King Lear*
by William Shakespeare

1927   *The Ring*
by Richard Wagner

1929   *The Birds*
by Aristophanes

1930   *Medea*
by Euripides

1932   *The Flying Dutchman*
by Richard Wagner

1933   *Love for Three Oranges*
by Carlo Gozzi

1933   *Hamlet*
by William Shakespeare

1934   *Le Cid*
by Pierre Corneille

1940   *As You Like It*
by William Shakespeare

1941   *The Book of Job*

1948   *Egmont*
by Johann Wolfgang von Goethe

[n.d.]   *Dinner for Queen Elizabeth II*
given by Pilgrims and English-Speaking Union

[n.d.]   *Judith's Garden*

Egmont, Curtain

Egmont, A meeting on a street corner

Egmont, Street scene

Egmont, Interior

Productions Designed by Donald Oenslager

March 31, 1925
Sooner and Later
a Dance Satire by Irene Lewisohn
Music by Emerson Whithorne
Directed by Irene Lewisohn
Produced by the Neighborhood Playhouse

May 12, 1925
A Bit O'Love
by John Galsworthy
Directed by Robert Milton
With O. P. Heggie
Produced by the Actor's Theatre

October 28, 1925
Celeste
by Helen Gaskill
Directed by Hubert Osborne
First performance of Department of Drama
Yale Theatre

November 30, 1925
Morals
by Ludwig Thoma
Acting Version by Sidney Howard
Directed by Dudley Digges
Produced by the Actor's Theatre

March 3, 1926
The Fall of the House of Usher
Adaptation by Frederick L. Day
Directed by George Pierce Baker
Yale Theatre

October 26, 1926
Plots and Playwrights
by Edward Massey
Directed by Hubert Osborne
Yale Theatre

December 10, 1926
The Patriarch
by Boyd M. Smith
Directed by George Pierce Baker
Opening of the University Theatre
Yale Theatre

February 3, 1927
Pinwheel
by Francis Edwards Faragoh
Directed by Irene and Alice Lewisohn
Produced by the Neighborhood Playhouse

April 29, 1927
Machiavelli
by Lemist Esler
Directed by Hubert Osborne
Yale Theatre

September 6, 1927
Good News
by Laurence Schwab and B. G. DeSylva
Music by DeSylva, Brown, and Henderson
Directed by Edgar MacGregor
Produced by Schwab and Mandel

December 13, 1927
Pueblo
by Covington Littleton
Directed by George Pierce Baker
Yale Theatre

March 25, 1928
L'Histoire du soldat
by Igor Stravinsky
Directed by Michio Ito
Conducted by Pierre Monteux
With Jacques Cartier and Tom Powers
Produced by the League of Composers

May 28, 1928
Anna
by Rudolph Lothar
Directed by Edgar MacGregor
With Judith Anderson and Lou Tellegen
Produced by Samuel Samach

May 28, 1928   *Brand*
by Henrik Ibsen
Directed by George Pierce Baker
Yale Theatre

November 19, 1928   *The New Moon*
by Oscar Hammerstein II, Frank Mandel, and
Laurence Schwab
Music by Sigmund Romberg
With Evelyn Herbert and Robert Halliday
Produced by Schwab and Mandel

January 9, 1929   *Follow Thru*
by Laurence Schwab and B. G. DeSylva
Music by DeSylva, Brown, and Henderson
Directed by Edgar MacGregor
With Jack Haley and Zelma O'Neal
Produced by Schwab and Mandel

May 20, 1929   *Stepping Out*
by Elmer Harris
Directed by Edgar MacGregor
Produced by Charles Dillingham

November 11, 1929   *Heads Up!*
by John McGowan and Paul G. Smith
Music and Lyrics by Rodgers and Hart
With Ray Bolger, Victor Moore, and
Betty Starbuck
Produced by Aarons and Freedley

December ?, 1929   *Fortnight*
Produced by David Wallace and Howard
Schnebbe

March 20, 1930   *The Searcher*
by Velona Pilcher
Directed by George Pierce Baker
Yale Theatre

October 14, 1930   *Girl Crazy*
by Guy Bolton and John McGowan
Music and Lyrics by George and Ira Gershwin
Directed by Alexander Leftwich
With Ethel Merman, Ginger Rogers, and
Willie Howard
Produced by Aarons and Freedley

November 8, 1930   *Trade Winds*
by Laurence Schwab
Directed by Lee Elmore
Produced by Schwab and Mandel

December 6, 1930   *Overture*
by William Bolitho
Directed by H. C. Potter
With Colin Clive, Barbara Robbins, and
Pat O'Brien
Produced by Bela Blau, Inc.

January 19, 1931   *You Said It*
Book by Jack Yellen and Sid Silvers
Music by Harold Arlen and Lyrics
by Jack Yellen
Directed by John Harwood
With Lou Holtz and Mary Lawlor
Produced by Yellen and Holtz

February 3, 1931   *Rock Me, Julie*
by Kenneth Raisbeck
Directed by James Light
With Helen Menken and Paul Muni
Produced by Green and Gensler

February 10, 1931   *America's Sweetheart*
Book by Herbert Fields
Music and Lyrics by Rodgers and Hart
Directed by Monty Woolley
With Jack Whiting and Gus Shy
Produced by Schwab and Mandel

March 30, 1931   *The Winter's Tale*
by William Shakespeare
Directed by George Pierce Baker
Yale Theatre

September 8, 1931   *Free for All*
by Oscar Hammerstein II and Laurence Schwab
Music by Richard Whiting
Directed by Oscar Hammerstein
Produced by Schwab and Mandel

October 5, 1931   *Singin' the Blues*
by John McGowan
Songs by Jimmy McHugh and Dorothy Fields
Directed by Bertram Harrison
Produced by Aarons and Freedley

October 27, 1931   *East Wind*
by Oscar Hammerstein II and Frank Mandel
Music by Sigmund Romberg
Directed by Oscar Hammerstein
Produced by Schwab and Mandel

November 14, 1931   *The Emperor Jones*
by Eugene O'Neill
Directed by George Pierce Baker
Yale Theatre

January 19, 1932   *Whistling in the Dark*
by Laurence Gross and Edward Childs Carpenter
Directed by Frank Craven
With Ernest Truex
Produced by Alexander McKaig

January 20, 1932   *Adam Had Two Sons*
by John McDermott
Directed by Melville Burke
Produced by Aarons and Freedley

May 24, 1932   *A Thousand Summers*
by Merrill Rogers
Directed by Shepard Traube
With Jane Cowl, Franchot Tone, and Osgood Perkins
Produced by Arch Selwyn

December 16, 1932   *The King's Coat*
by Fred R. Kleibacker Jr.
Directed by George Pierce Baker
Yale Theatre

March 6, 1933   *Forsaking All Others*
by Edward Roberts and Frank Cavett
Directed by Thomas Mitchell
With Tallulah Bankhead and Fred Keating
Produced by Arch Selwyn

May 29, 1933   *Uncle Tom's Cabin*
Dramatized by G. D. Aiken from the Novel by Harriet Beecher Stowe
Directed by Earle Booth
With Otis Skinner, Fay Bainter, and All-Star Cast
Produced by The Players — Twelfth Annual Revival

October 18, 1933   *Keeper of the Keys*
by Valentine Davies
With William Harrigan
Directed and Produced by Sigourney Thayer

December 18, 1933   *Venice Preserved*
by Thomas Otway
Directed by Alexander Dean
Yale Theatre

January 1, 1934   *Jezebel*
by Owen Davis
With Miriam Hopkins
Directed and Produced by Guthrie McClintic

January 13, 1934   *Salome*
Opera by Richard Strauss
Directed by Wilhelm Von Wymetal Jr.
Conducted by Artur Bodanzky
With Goeta Ljunberg
Produced by the Metropolitan Opera Association

March 17, 1934   *Sweet Bells Jangled*
by Reginald Lawrence
Directed by William Schorr
With Jane Cowl
Produced by Seldon Bennett and Shepard Traube

May 1, 1934   *Lady from the Sea*
by Henrik Ibsen
Directed by John Houseman
Produced by Nathan Zatkin

August 6, 1934

Hide and Seek
by Richard Macaulay and Laurence Schwab
Directed by Robert Sinclair
With Burgess Meredith and Lou Polan
Produced by Laurence Schwab

October 2, 1934

Divided by Three
by Margaret Leech and Beatrice Kaufman
With Judith Anderson, James Stewart, and
Hedda Hopper
Directed and Produced by Guthrie McClintic

October 6, 1934

Dance with Your Gods
by Kenneth Perkins and Roy Hargrave
Directed by Robert Sinclair
Produced by Laurence Schwab

October 19, 1934

Tristan and Isolde
by Richard Wagner
Directed by Herbert Graf
Conducted by Fritz Reiner
With Hans Grahl and Marga Dannenberg
Produced by the Philadelphia Orchestra Association

October 30, 1934

The Farmer Takes a Wife
by Frank Elser and Marc Connelly
Directed by Marc Connelly
With Henry Fonda and June Walker
Produced by Max Gordon

November 21, 1934

Anything Goes
by Guy Bolton and P. G. Wodehouse
Music by Cole Porter
Directed by Howard Lindsay
With Ethel Merman, Victor Moore, and
William Gaxton
Produced by Vinton Freedley

November 28, 1934

Gold Eagle Guy
by Melvin Levy
Directed by Lee Strasberg
With J. Edward Bromberg, Alexander Kirkland,
Stella Adler, Sanford Meisner, Elia
Kazan, and Clifford Odets
Produced by the Group Theatre, Inc.

November 30, 1934

Der Rosenkavalier
by Richard Strauss
Directed by Herbert Graf
Conducted by Fritz Reiner
With Lotte Lehman
Produced by the Philadelphia Orchestra
Association

December 24, 1934

Christmas Oratorio
by Johann Sebastian Bach
Conducted by Macklin Marrow
With Lillian Gish
Produced by Delos Chappell

February 15, 1935

Hollywood Holiday
by Kay Kenney and Douglas Gilmore
Directed by Thomas Mitchell
With Bebe Daniels and Ben Lyon
Produced by Mayfair Productions Inc.

April 29, 1935

Something Gay
by Adelaide Heilbron
Directed by Thomas Mitchell
With Tallulah Bankhead
Produced by the Messrs. Shubert

September 30, 1935

The Ascending Dragon
by Frederick Jackson
Directed by Ira Hards
With Cardini, the Magician
Produced by Camillo Aldao

October 11, 1935

Sweet Mystery of Life
by Richard Maibaum, Michael Wallach, and
George Haight
With Gene Lockhart
Directed and Produced by Herman Shumlin

November 26, 1935

First Lady
by Katherine Dayton and George S. Kaufman
Directed by George Kaufman
With Jane Cowl
Produced by Sam H. Harris

December 27, 1935   *Tapestry in Gray*
by Martin Flavin
Directed by Marion Gering
With Elissa Landi and Melvyn Douglas
Produced by B. P. Schulberg

———, 1935   *Land of the Living*
by Marc Connelly
Designed for Bela Blau
Unproduced

February 3, 1936   *Russet Mantle*
by Lynn Riggs
Directed by Alexander Dean
Produced by Jerome Mayer

September 21, 1936   *Timber House*
by John Boruff
Directed by J. Edward Shugrue
Produced by Charles E. Fiske and Paul Hammond

October 22, 1936   *Stage Door*
by George S. Kaufman and Edna Ferber
Directed by Mr. Kaufman
With Margaret Sullavan, Lee Patrick, and
Onslow Stevens
Produced by Sam H. Harris

October 23, 1936   *Ten Million Ghosts*
by Sidney Kingsley
With George Coulouris and Orson Welles
Directed and Produced by Mr. Kingsley

October 28, 1936   *Sweet River: An Adaptation of
Harriet Beecher Stowe's
Uncle Tom's Cabin*
by George Abbott
Directed and Produced by Mr. Abbott

November 12, 1936   *Matrimony Pfd.*
by Louis Verneuil
Adapted by Grace George and James Forbes
Directed by José Ruben
With Grace George
Produced by William A. Brady

November 16, 1936   *Red, Hot and Blue!*
by Howard Lindsay and Russel Crouse
Music by Cole Porter
Directed by Mr. Lindsay
With Jimmy Durante, Ethel Merman, and Bob
Hope
Produced by Vinton Freedley

November 19, 1936   *Johnny Johnson*
by Paul Green
Music by Kurt Weill
Directed by Lee Strasberg
Produced by the Group Theatre, Inc.

November 20, 1936   *200 Were Chosen*
by E. P. Conkle
Directed by Worthington Miner
Produced by Sidney Harmon and the Actor's
Repertory Company

December 14, 1936   *You Can't Take It With You*
by George S. Kaufman and Moss Hart
Directed by Mr. Kaufman
With Josephine Hull and Henry Travers
Produced by Sam H. Harris

March 17, 1937   *Le Bourgeois Gentilhomme*
by Molière
Directed by Halsted Welles
Yale Theatre

April 1, 1937   *Le Pauvre Matelot*
Text by Jean Cocteau
Music by Darius Milhaud
Directed by Ernst Joseph Maria Lert
Conducted by Fritz Reiner
Produced by Curtis Institute of Music

April 1, 1937   *Amelia Goes to the Ball*
Music and Text by Gian-Carlo Menotti
Directed by Ernst Joseph Maria Lert
Conducted by Fritz Reiner
Produced by Curtis Institute of Music

April 7, 1937

Miss Quis
by Ward Morehouse
Directed by Bertram Harrison
With Jessie Royce Landis
Produced by Vinton Freedley

November 2, 1937

I'd Rather Be Right
by George S. Kaufman and Moss Hart
Music and Lyrics by Rodgers and Hart
Directed by Mr. Kaufman
With George M. Cohan
Produced by Sam H. Harris

November 18, 1937

Robin Landing
by Stanley Young
Directed by Halsted Welles
With Ian Keith and Louis Calhern
Produced by Sidney Harmon and
T. Edward Hambleton

November 23, 1937

Of Mice and Men
by John Steinbeck
Directed by George S. Kaufman
With Broderick Crawford, Wallace Ford, and
Claire Luce
Produced by Sam H. Harris

December 7, 1937

Edna His Wife
Dramatized by Cornelia Otis Skinner from the
Novel by Margaret Ayer Barnes
Played and Produced by Miss Skinner

December 22, 1937

Otello
by Giuseppe Verdi
Directed by Herbert Graf
Conducted by Ettore Panizza
With Giovanni Martinelli and Lawrence Tibbett
Produced by the Metropolitan Opera Associa-
tion

December 27, 1937

A Doll's House
by Henrik Ibsen
Acting Version by Thornton Wilder
Directed by Jed Harris
With Ruth Gordon, Dennis King, and Paul
Lukas
First Produced by Central City Opera Associa-
tion
Subsequently produced by Jed Harris

March 3, 1938

Amelia Goes to the Ball
Music and Text by Gian-Carlo Menotti
Directed by Leopold Sachse
Conducted by Ettore Panizza
With Muriel Dickson and John Brownlee
Produced by the Metropolitan Opera Associa-
tion

March 7, 1938

I Am My Youth
by Ernest Pascal and Edwin Blum
Directed and Produced by Alfred deLiagre Jr.

March 21, 1938

Spring Thaw
by Clare Kummer
Directed by Eddie Sobol and Arthur Hopkins
With Roland Young
Produced by Max Gordon

April 18, 1938

The Circle
by Somerset Maugham
Directed by Bretaigne Windust
With Tallulah Bankhead and Grace George
Produced by William A. Brady

October 5, 1938

The Good
by Chester Erskin
Directed by Mr. Erskin
With Frances Starr and Robert Keith
Produced by Norman and Irvin Pincus

October 8, 1938

The Fabulous Invalid
by Moss Hart and George S. Kaufman
Directed by Mr. Kaufman
Produced by Sam H. Harris

The Fabulous Invalid, Solinsky's Alexandria Theatre

The Fabulous Invalid, Oenslager researching

The Fabulous Invalid, At the drawing board

154

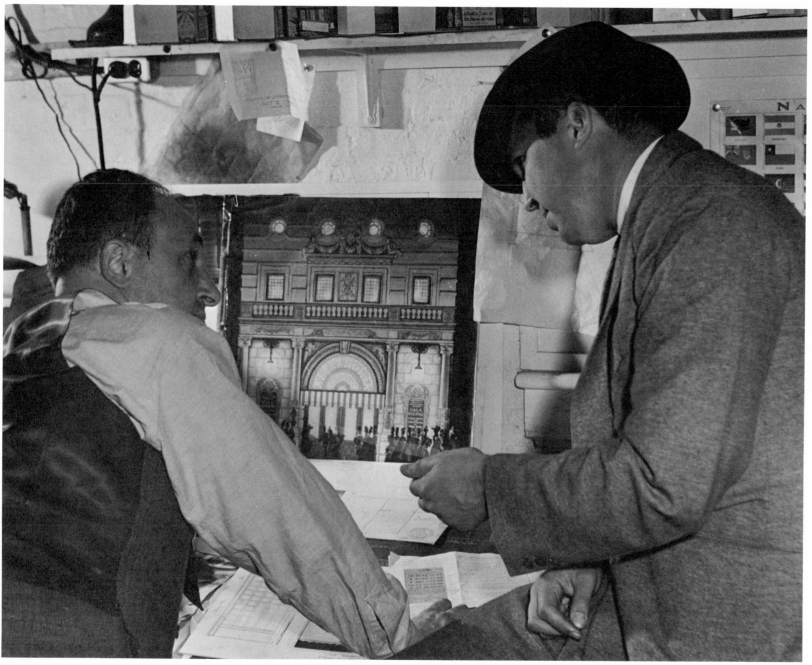

The Fabulous Invalid, In conference

The Fabulous Invalid, Scenery being painted at Triangle Studios

The Fabulous Invalid, The "load in" at the Broadhurst Theatre

October 18, 1938

A Woman's a Fool — To Be Clever
by Dorothy Bennett and Link Hannah
Directed by Robert Milton
Produced by John J. Wildberg

November 10, 1938

The Flying Ginzburgs
by Max Liebman and Allen Boretz
Directed by Melville Burke
With Hume Cronyn
Produced by Vinton Freedley

January 21, 1939

The American Way
by George S. Kaufman and Moss Hart
Directed by Mr. Kaufman and Hassard Short
With Fredric March and Florence Eldridge
Produced by Sam H. Harris and Max Gordon

January 21, 1939

The Birds Stop Singing
by Lenore Coffee
Directed by William Miles
With Ruth Gordon and Walter Abel
Produced by John Golden

February 21, 1939

Off to Buffalo
by Max Liebman and Allen Boretz
Directed by Melville Burke
Produced by Albert Lewis

March 20, 1939

Candida
by George Bernard Shaw
Directed by George Somnes
With Cornelia Otis Skinner
Produced by Skinner Theatricals, Inc.

June 20, 1939

From Vienna
Musical Review by the Refugee Artists Group
Directed by Herbert Berghof
Produced by Refugee Artists Group

October 16, 1939

Skylark
by Samson Raphaelson
Directed by Mr. Raphaelson
With Gertrude Lawrence
Produced by John Golden

October 16, 1939

The Man Who Came to Dinner
by Moss Hart and George S. Kaufman
Directed by Mr. Kaufman
With Monty Woolley
Produced by Sam H. Harris

October 30, 1939

Margin for Error
by Clare Boothe Luce
Directed by Otto Preminger
With Otto Preminger, Sam Levene, Bramwell
Fletcher, and Bert Lytell
Produced by Aldrich and Myers

November 24, 1939

I Know What I Like
by Justin Sturm
Directed by Auriol Lee
Produced by T. Edward Hambleton and
Richard Skinner

December 13, 1939

Prometheus Bound
by Aeschylus
Translated by Edith Hamilton
Directed by Constance Welsh
Yale Theatre

December 13, 1939

The Merchant
by Plautus
Adapted by Arthur Wilmurt
Directed by Frank McMullan
Yale Theatre

January 24, 1940

Young Couple Wanted
by Arthur Wilmurt
Directed by Martin Gabel
Produced by Jerome Mayer

January 31, 1940

My Dear Children
by Catherine Turney and Jerry Horwin
Directed by Otto Preminger
With John Barrymore
Produced by Aldrich and Myers

October 28, 1940

The White-Haired Boy
by Charles Martin and Beatrice Kaufman
Directed and Produced by George Abbott

November 11, 1940	*Beverly Hills* by Lynn Starling and Howard Green Directed by Otto Preminger Produced by Laurence Schwab and Mr. Preminger
December 7, 1940	*Out West It's Different* by Bella and Samuel Spewack Directed by Mr. Levene and Mr. Spewack Produced by Max Gordon
December 17, 1940	*Retreat to Pleasure* by Irwin Shaw Directed by Harold Clurman Produced by the Group Theatre, Inc.
December 20, 1940	*The Old Foolishness* by Paul Vincent Carroll Directed by Rachel Crothers Produced by John Golden
December 26, 1940	*My Sister Eileen* by Joseph Fields and Jerome Chodorov Directed by George S. Kaufman With Shirley Booth Produced by Max Gordon
January 2, 1941	*The Lady Who Came to Stay* by Kenneth White With Mady Christians and Mildred Natwick Directed and Produced by Guthrie McClintic
March 11, 1941	*The Doctor's Dilemma* by George Bernard Shaw Directed by Guthrie McClintic With Katharine Cornell and Raymond Massey Produced by Katharine Cornell
March 31, 1941	*Claudia* by Rose Franken Directed by Rose Franken With Donald Cook and Dorothy McGuire Produced by John Golden
March 1941	*As You Like It* by William Shakespeare With Katharine Hepburn Designed for the Theatre Guild; Unproduced
September 30, 1941	*Mr. Big* by Arthur Sheekman and Margaret Shane With Hume Cronyn Directed and Produced by George S. Kaufman
October 6, 1941	*Father's Day* by Frances Goodrich and Albert Hackett Directed by Arthur Sircom With Charles Butterworth Produced by Aldrich and Myers
November 10, 1941	*Spring Again* by Isabel Leighton and Bertram Bloch With Grace George and C. Aubrey Smith Directed and Produced by Guthrie McClintic
November 12, 1941	*Theatre* by Guy Bolton and Somerset Maugham With Cornelia Otis Skinner Directed and Produced by John Golden
December 22, 1941	*Pie in the Sky* by Bernadine Angus Directed by Edgar MacGregor Produced by Mr. MacGregor
December 27, 1941	*Portrait of a Lady* by Alexander King and Chester Erskin Directed by Mr. Erskin With Ruth Gordon Produced by Aldrich and Myers
January 19, 1942	*Rose Burke* by Henri Bernstein Directed by Guthrie McClintic With Katharine Cornell, Jean-Pierre Aumont, and Philip Merivale Produced by Katharine Cornell

February 5, 1942
Flowers of Virtue
by Marc Connelly
Directed by Mr. Connelly
With Frank Craven
Produced by Cheryl Crawford

May 4, 1942
Punch and Julia
by George Batson
With Jane Cowl
Directed and Produced by Guthrie McClintic

December 26, 1945
Pygmalion
by George Bernard Shaw
Directed by Cedric Hardwicke
With Gertrude Lawrence and Raymond Massey
Produced by Theatre, Inc.

February 4, 1946
Born Yesterday
by Garson Kanin
Directed by Mr. Kanin
With Judy Holliday and Paul Douglas
Produced by Max Gordon

March 7, 1946
Three to Make Ready
by Nancy Hamilton
Music by Morgan Lewis
Directed by John Murray Anderson
With Ray Bolger and Gordon McRae
Produced by Stanley Gilkey and Barbara Payne

May 8, 1946
On Whitman Avenue
by Maxine Wood
Directed by Margo Jones
With Canada Lee
Produced by Canada Lee and Mark Marvin

July 6, 1946
The Abduction from the Seraglio
by Wolfgang Amadeus Mozart
Directed by Herbert Graf
Conducted by Emil Cooper
With Eleanor Steber
Produced by Central City Opera Association

July 7, 1946
La Traviata
by Giuseppe Verdi
Directed by Herbert Graf
Conducted by Emil Cooper
With Florence Quartaro and John B. McCormack
Produced by Central City Opera Association

October 16, 1946
Loco
by Dale Eunson and Katherine Albert
Directed and Produced by Jed Harris

October 29, 1946
Present Laughter
by Noel Coward
With Clifton Webb
Directed and Produced by John C. Wilson

November 19, 1946
The Fatal Weakness
by George Kelly
Directed by Mr. Kelly
With Ina Claire
Produced by the Theatre Guild, Inc.

November 25, 1946
The Temporary Mrs. Smith
by Jacqueline Susann and Beatrice Cole
Directed by Jessie Royce Landis
Produced by Vinton Freedley

November 29, 1946
The Abduction from the Seraglio
by Wolfgang Amadeus Mozart
Directed by Herbert Graf
Conducted by Emil Cooper
With Eleanor Steber
Produced by the Metropolitan Opera Association

December 3, 1946
Years Ago
by Ruth Gordon
Directed by Garson Kanin
With Fredric March and Florence Eldridge
Produced by Max Gordon

December 9, 1946

Park Avenue
by Nunnally Johnson and George S. Kaufman
Music by Arthur Schwartz, Lyrics by
Ira Gershwin
Directed by Mr. Kaufman
With Leonora Corbett and Arthur Margetson
Produced by Max Gordon

December 11, 1946

Land's End
by Thomas Job
Directed by Robert Lewis
With Shirley Booth
Produced by Paul Feigay

January 23, 1947

Washington Square
by Ruth Goodman and Augustus Goetz
Directed by Jack Minster
Produced by Oscar Serlin

February 18, 1947

The Greatest of These
by Max Wylie
Directed by Eddie Dowling
Produced by Frank Satenstein

March 19, 1947

The Eagle Has Two Heads
by Jean Cocteau
With Tallulah Bankhead and Helmut Dantine
Directed and Produced by John C. Wilson

April 16, 1947

Message for Margaret
by James Parish
Directed by Elliott Nugent
With Mady Christians and Miriam Hopkins
Produced by Stanley Gilkey and Barbara Payne

May 14, 1947

Portrait in Black
by Ivan Goff and Ben Roberts
Directed by Reginald Denham
With Claire Luce, Donald Cook, and
Sidney Blackmer
Produced by David Lowe and Edgar Luckenbach

July 4, 1947

Martha
by Friedrich von Flotow
Directed by Herbert Graf
Conducted by Emil Cooper
With Frances Greer and James Pease
Produced by Central City Opera Association

July 4, 1947

Fidelio
by Ludwig van Beethoven
Directed by Herbert Graf
Conducted by Emil Cooper
With Regina Resnik and Brian Sullivan
Produced by Central City Opera Association

September 30, 1947

How I Wonder
by Donald Ogden Stewart
Directed by Garson Kanin
With Raymond Massey
Produced by Ruth Gordon and Garson Kanin

November 18, 1947

Eastward in Eden
by Dorothy Gardner
Directed by Ellen Van Volkenburg
With Beatrice Straight
Produced by Nancy Stern

December 11, 1947

Angel in the Wings
Sketches by Hank Ladd, Ted Luce, and
the Hartmans
Words and Music by Bob Hilliard and
Carl Sigman
Directed by John Kennedy
With Grace and Paul Hartman
Produced by Marjorie and Sherman Ewing

January 16, 1948

The Men We Marry
by Elisabeth Cobb and Herschel Williams
Directed by Martin Manulis
With Shirley Booth
Produced by Edgar Luckenbach

July 2, 1948

Tales of Hoffman
by Jacques Offenbach
Directed by Herbert Graf
Conducted by Emil Cooper
With Mario Berini and Igor Gorin
Produced by Central City Opera Association

July 3, 1948   *Cosi Fan Tutte*
by Wolfgang Amadeus Mozart
Directed by Herbert Graf
Conducted by Emil Cooper
With Anne Bollinger
Produced by Central City Opera Association

September 23, 1948   *Town House*
by Gertrude Tonkonogy
Directed by George S. Kaufman
Produced by Max Gordon

October 18, 1948   *The Leading Lady*
by Ruth Gordon
Directed by Garson Kanin
With Ruth Gordon, Ian Keith, and
Mildred Dunnock
Produced by Victor Samrock and William Fields

October 20, 1948   *Life with Mother*
by Howard Lindsay and Russel Crouse
Directed by Guthrie McClintic
With Dorothy Stickney and Howard Lindsay
Produced by Oscar Serlin

November 17, 1948   *Goodbye My Fancy*
by Fay Kanin
Directed by Sam Wanamaker
With Madeleine Carroll, Shirley Booth, and
Conrad Nagel
Produced by Michael Kanin in association with
Aldrich and Myers

January 12, 1949   *Smile of the World*
by Garson Kanin
Directed by Mr. Kanin
With Ruth Gordon and Otto Kruger
Produced by the Playwright's Company

March 8, 1949   *At War with the Army*
by James B. Allardice
Directed by Ezra Stone
Produced by Henry May and Jerome Rosenfeld
in association with Charles McCallum

November 16, 1949   *The Father*
by August Strindberg
Directed by Raymond Massey
With Raymond Massey and Mady Christians
Produced by Richard Krakeur and Robert
Joseph

December 22, 1949   *The Rat Race*
by Garson Kanin
Directed by Daniel Mann and Mr. Kanin
With Betty Field
Produced by Leland Hayward

December 26, 1949   *The Velvet Glove*
by Rosemary Casey
With Grace George and Walter Hampden
Directed and Produced by Guthrie McClintic

May 18, 1950   *The Liar*
by Carlo Goldoni
Book by Edward Eager and Alfred Drake
Music and Lyrics by John Mundy and Edward
Eager
Directed by Alfred Drake
With William Eythe and Melville Cooper
Produced by Dorothy Willard and Thomas
Hammond

August 17, 1950   *The Live Wire*
by Garson Kanin
Directed by Mr. Kanin
Produced by Michael Todd

October 9, 1950   *Springboard to Nowhere*
by Alexander Lidor
Directed and Produced by Eddie Dowling

January 2, 1951   *Second Threshold*
by Philip Barry, with Revisions by
Robert Sherwood
With Clive Brook
Directed and Produced by Alfred deLiagre Jr.

January 28, 1951   *Peer Gynt*
by Henrik Ibsen
Directed by Lee Strasberg
With John Garfield
Produced by ANTA–Cheryl Crawford and
Roger Stevens

February 15, 1951   *The Small Hours*
by George S. Kaufman and Leueen MacGrath
Directed by Mr. Kaufman
With Dorothy Stickney
Produced by Max Gordon

July 12, 1951   *The Beautiful Galatea*
by Franz von Suppé
Directed by Alfred deLiagre Jr.
Conducted by Tibor Kozma
Produced by Central City Opera Association

July 12, 1951   *Amelia Goes to the Ball*
Music and Libretto by Gian-Carlo Menotti
Directed by Alfred deLiagre Jr.
Conducted by Tibor Kozma
With Eleanor Steber
Produced by Central City Opera Association

August 4, 1951   *The Constant Wife*
by W. Somerset Maugham
Directed by Guthrie McClintic
With Katharine Cornell, Grace George and
Brian Aherne
Produced by Central City Opera Association
Produced by Katharine Cornell in New York,
December 8, 1951

March 4, 1952   *Paris '90*
by Cornelia Otis Skinner
Music and Lyrics by Kay Swift
Produced and Played by Miss Skinner

April 22, 1952   *Candida*
by George Bernard Shaw
Directed by Norris Houghton and Herman
Shumlin
With Olivia de Havilland
Produced by Thomas Hammond

April 23, 1952   *To be Continued*
by William Marchant
With Dorothy Stickney
Produced and Directed by Guthrie McClintic

June 28, 1952   *La Bohème*
by Giacomo Puccini
Directed by Frank St. Leger
Conducted by Tibor Kozma
With Ann Ayars
Produced by Central City Opera Association

February 17, 1953   *Comedy on the Bridge*
by Bohuslav Martinu
Music Director Arthur Frantz
Directed by Elemer Nagy
Yale Theatre

February 17, 1953   *Dido and Aeneas*
Opera by Henry Purcell
Directed by Elemer Nagy
Yale Theatre

April 2, 1953   *Horses in Midstream*
by Andrew Rosenthal
Directed by Cedric Hardwicke
With Diana Lynn and Cedric Hardwicke
Produced by Gilbert Miller and
Donald Oenslager

June 27, 1953   *Carmen*
by Georges Bizet
Directed by Herbert Graf
Conducted by Kurt Adler
Produced by Central City Opera Association

November 11, 1953   *Sabrina Fair*
by Samuel Taylor
Directed by H. C. Potter
With Margaret Sullavan and Joseph Cotten
Produced by the Playwright's Company

November 18, 1953   *Escapade*
by Roger MacDougall
With Brian Aherne and Ursula Jeans
Directed and Produced by Alfred deLiagre Jr.

December 1, 1953   *Madam, Will You Walk*
by Sidney Howard
Directed by Hume Cronyn and Norman Lloyd
With Hume Cronyn and Jessica Tandy
Produced by the Phoenix Theatre

December 16, 1953   *The Prescott Proposals*
by Howard Lindsay and Russel Crouse
Directed by Mr. Lindsay
With Katharine Cornell
Produced by Leland Hayward

January 19, 1954   *Coriolanus*
by William Shakespeare
Directed by John Houseman
With Robert Ryan, John Emery, and
Mildred Natwick
Produced by the Phoenix Theatre

September 15, 1954   *Dear Charles*
Adapted by Alan Melville
Directed by Edmund Baylies
With Tallulah Bankhead
Produced by Aldrich and Myers

October 6, 1955   *The Wooden Dish*
by Edmund Morris
Directed by Louis Calhern
With Louis Calhern
Produced by Armand Deutsch

October 17, 1955   *A Roomful of Roses*
by Edith Sommer
Directed by Guthrie McClintic
With Patricia Neal
Produced by Guthrie McClintic and
Stanley Gilkey

November 24, 1955   *Janus*
by Carolyn Green
Directed by Reginald Denham
With Margaret Sullavan, Robert Preston, and
Claude Dauphin
Produced by Alfred deLiagre Jr.

November 23, 1955   *A Quiet Place*
by Julian Claman
Directed by Delbert Mann
With Tyrone Power and Leora Dana
Produced by the Playwright's Company

———, 1955   *Readings from the Bible by Judith Anderson,*
a television Program

July 7, 1956   *The Ballad of Baby Doe*
by Douglas Moore
Libretto by John La Touche
Directed by Hanya Holm
Conducted by Emerson Buckley
With Martha Lipton, Dolores Wilson, and
Walter Cassell
Produced by Central City Opera Association

October 30, 1956   *Major Barbara*
by George Bernard Shaw
Directed by Charles Laughton
With Mr. Laughton, Cornelia Otis Skinner,
Glynis Johns, Eli Wallach,
and Burgess Meredith
Produced by Robert Joseph and
Producer's Theatre

July 5, 1957   *The Man in the Dog Suit*
by William Wright and Albert Beich
Directed by Ralph Nelson
With Hume Cronyn and Jessica Tandy
Produced by Mr. Cronyn

September 25, 1957   *Four Winds*
by Thomas W. Phipps
Directed by Guthrie McClintic
With Ann Todd
Produced by Worthington Miner and Kenneth
Wagg

October 8, 1957   *Mary Stuart*
by Friedrich von Schiller
Directed by Tyrone Guthrie
With Eva LeGallienne and Irene Worth
Produced by the Phoenix Theatre

October 16, 1957 — *Nature's Way*
by Hermann Wouk
Directed by Alfred deLiagre Jr.
With Orson Bean and Betsy von Furstenberg
Produced by Alfred deLiagre Jr.

December 11, 1957 — *A Shadow of My Enemy*
by Sol Stein
Directed by Daniel Petrie
With Ed Begley and Raymond Scott
Produced by Nick Mayo

April 22, 1958 — *"J. B."*
by Archibald MacLeish
Directed by F. C. Canfield
Produced by Yale Drama School

August 2, 1958 — *And Perhaps Happiness*
by Thomas Hornsby Ferrill
Directed by Edwin Levy
With K. T. Stevens, Hugh Marlowe, and
Barbara O'Neill
Produced by Central City Opera Association

October 15, 1958 — *The Girls in 509*
by Howard Teichmann
Directed by Bretaigne Windust
With Peggy Wood and Imogene Coca
Produced by Alfred deLiagre Jr.

October 22, 1958 — *The Pleasure of His Company*
by Cornelia Otis Skinner and Samuel Taylor
Directed by Cyril Ritchard
With Miss Skinner, Mr. Ritchard, and
Charlie Ruggles
Produced by the Playwright's Company

October 29, 1958 — *The Marriage Go Round*
by Leslie Stevens
Directed by Joseph Anthony
With Claudette Colbert and Charles Boyer
Produced by Paul Gregory

February 16, 1959 — *A Majority of One*
by Leonard Spigelgass
Directed by Dore Schary
With Gertrude Berg and Sir Cedric Hardwicke
Produced by Dore Schary and the Theatre Guild

July 18, 1959 — *Orpheus and Eurydice*
by Christoph Willibald von Glück
Directed by Hanya Holm
Conducted by Oivin Fjeldstadt
With Kerstin Meyer and Mary Costa
Produced by the Vancouver International
Festival for Queen Elizabeth II

October 2, 1959 — *The Mikado*
by W. S. Gilbert and Arthur Sullivan
Staged by Dorothy Raedler
Conducted by Robert Irving
Produced by the New York City Opera Company

October 14, 1959 — *The Pink Jungle*
by Leslie Stevens
Directed by Joseph Anthony
With Ginger Rogers and Agnes Moorehead
Produced by Paul Gregory

November 4, 1959 — *The Highest Tree*
by Dore Schary
Directed by Mr. Schary
With Kenneth McKenna
Produced by Mr. Schary and the American
Theatre Guild

March 17, 1960 — *Dear Liar*
Comedy of Letters Adapted to Stage by Jerome
Kilty from Correspondence of George
Bernard Shaw and Mrs. Patrick Campbell
Directed by Mr. Kilty
With Katharine Cornell and Brian Aherne
Produced by Guthrie McClintic in Association
With Sol Hurok

September 30, 1960 — *Orfeo*
Music by Claudio Monteverdi
Libretto by Alessandro Stiggio
Staged by Christopher West
Conducted by Leopold Stokowski
Produced by New York City Opera Company

September 30, 1960 — *The Prisoner*
Music and Libretto by Luigi
Dallapiccola
Staged by Christopher West
Conducted by Leopold Stokowski
Produced by New York City Opera Company
(On double bill with *Orfeo*)

May 25, 1961 — *A Far Country*
by Henry Denker
Directed by Alfred Ryder
With Kim Stanley and Steve Hill
Produced by Roger L. Stevens

May 25, 1961 — *A Call on Kuprin*
by Jerome Lawrence and Robert Lee,
Based on the Novel by Maurice Edelman
Directed by George Abbott
With Jeffrey Lynn and Eugenie Leontovich
Produced by Griffith and Prince

October 5, 1961 — *Blood, Sweat and Stanley Poole*
by James and William Goldman
Directed by Jerome Chodorov
With Darren McGavin and Peter Fonda
Produced by Roger L. Stevens

October 12, 1961 — *The Wings of the Dove*
Music by Douglas Moore,
Libretto by Ethan Ayer
Staged by Christopher West
Conducted by Julius Rudel
Costumes by Patton Campbell
Produced by New York City Opera Company

December 25, 1961 — *First Love*
by Samuel Taylor
Directed by Alfred Lunt
With Lili Darvas and Hugh O'Brien
Produced by Roger L. Stevens

April 12, 1962 — *Venus at Large*
by Henry Denker
Produced by Joel Schenker

October 22, 1962 — *Il Ballo Delle Ingrate*
by Monteverdi and
Persephone
by Stravinsky
Directed by Edwin Levy
Conducted by Thomas Scherman
Produced by the Concert Opera Association

September 18, 1963 — *The Irregular Verb to Love*
by Hugh and Margaret Williams
Directed by Cyril Ritchard
With Cyril Ritchard and Claudette Colbert
Produced by Alfred deLiagre Jr.

October 10, 1963 — *A Case of Libel*
by Henry Denker, based on Louis Nizer's
My Life in Court
Directed by Sam Wanamaker
With Van Heflin
Produced by Roger L. Stevens and Joel Schenker

June 27, 1964 — *Madama Butterfly*
by Giacomo Puccini
Directed by Christopher West
Produced by Central City Opera Association

July 3, 1964 — *The Lady from Colorado* (Première)
by Robert Ward
Libretto by Bernard Stambler
Directed by Christopher West
Produced by Central City Opera Association

December 1, 1964 — *One by One*
by Dore Schary
Directed by Mr. Schary
Produced by Mr. Schary and Walter Hyman

June 25, 1966 — *Carmen*
by Georges Bizet
Directed by James Lucas
Produced by Central City Opera Association

July 2, 1966	*The Italian Lady from Algiers* by Gioacchimo Rossini Directed by James Lucas Produced by Central City Opera Association	December 14, 1967	*Spofford* by Herman Shumlin Directed by Mr. Shumlin Produced by Zev Bufman
October 9, 1966	*Tosca* by Giacomo Puccini Directed by Tito Capobianco Conducted by Anton Guadagno Produced by New York City Opera Association	January 31, 1968	*Avanti!* by Samuel Taylor Directed by Nigel Patrick Produced by Morris Jacobs and Jerome Whyte in Association with Richard Rodgers
February 13, 1967	*Love in E Flat* by Norman Krasna Directed by George Seaton Produced by Alfred deLiagre Jr.	April 6, 1968	*Don Carlos* by Giuseppe Verdi Directed by Tito Capobianco Conducted by Victor Alessandro Produced by HemisFair '68, the Tobin Foundation, and San Antonio Symphony
February 17, 1967	*Der Rosenkavalier* by Richard Strauss Directed by Otto Erhardt Conducted by Julius Rudel Produced by New York City Opera Association	March 4, 1969	*The Wrong Way to Light a Bulb* by Leonard Spigelgass Directed by Stephen Porter Produced by Elliot Martin
June 18, 1967	*Antigone* by Jean Anouilh Directed by Jerome Kilty Performed at American Shakespeare Festival Theatre & Academy at Stratford, Connecticut	November, 1974	*Good News* (Revival) Produced by Harry Rigby
June 24, 1967	*The Merry Widow* by Franz Lehar Directed by James Lucas Produced by Central City Opera Association	———, 1974	*Mikado* (Revival) Directed and Choreographed by Jack Eddleman With James Billings, Gary Glage, Diana Sogiero Produced by New York City Opera Association
July 1, 1967	*Don Pasquale* by Gaetano Donizetti Directed by James Lucas Produced by Central City Opera Association		
July 8, 1967	*The Masked Ball (Un Ballo in Masch-era)* by Giuseppe Verdi Directed by James Lucas Produced by Central City Opera Association		

Index

Numbers in italics refer to pages on which illustrations are found.